the
SECRET LANGUAGE
of Star Signs

DECODING THE HIDDEN LANGUAGE OF ASTROLOGY

Jane Struthers

METRO BOOKS

NEW YORK

METRO BOOKS
New York

An Imprint of Sterling Publishing
387 Park Avenue South
New York, NY 10016

Conceived, designed, and produced by
Quid Publishing
Level 4 Sheridan House
114 Western Road
Hove BN3 1DD
England
www.quidpublishing.com

Design by Ali Walper

ISBN 978-1-4351-5073-7

For information about custom editions, special sales, and premium
and corporate purchases, please contact Sterling Special Sales at 800-805-5489
or specialsales@sterlingpublishing.com.

Manufactured in China

1 3 5 7 9 10 8 6 4 2

www.sterlingpublishing.com

CONTENTS

INTRODUCTION

Astrology is the art of studying the positions of the planets, and the relationships between them, which are calculated for a particular time, day, and place. The resulting natal chart or horoscope can be set for anything from the birth of a child to the purchase of a car, and much else besides. The distribution of the planets around the chart and the way they relate to one another describes the event concerned, including its potentials and pitfalls. Interpreting a natal chart takes skill and experience, but even simple star sign astrology can reveal a tremendous amount about a person's character. The only information you need is the person's date of birth, as this will tell you which star sign they belong to. Someone whose birthday falls on February 10, for instance, was born under the sign of Aquarius.

FOLLOWING THE SUN

Star signs are also known as Sun signs because they are the twelve zodiac signs through which the Sun moves during its apparent journey around the Earth each year. The Moon and the planets in our solar system also follow this path, which is called the ecliptic. It is a narrow band in the sky that lies at an angle of just over 23° to the celestial equator (a projection of the Earth's equator). For millennia, astronomers and astrologers have figuratively divided this band into twelve segments of 30° each, so they can track the precise progress of all the heavenly bodies as they move through the sky.

The astrological year begins on or around March 21, at the time of the vernal equinox, when the Sun enters the sign of Aries. The precise time and date of this event changes from year to year, as is the case with the Sun's entry into each of the other eleven signs. This is why there is no definitive date for the end of one star

sign and the start of the next. If you were born on the cusp between two signs, you can discover your exact star sign by consulting an astrologer, looking in a compendium of planetary positions (known as an ephemeris), or by finding the information in one of the online sites that provides free natal charts.

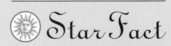

The path of the ecliptic, around which the Sun and planets travel, is a circle and therefore consists of 360°. There are twelve zodiac signs, so the path of the ecliptic is symbolically divided into equal segments of 30° each.

THE HISTORY OF ASTROLOGY

Man has been watching the progress of the planets through the sky for many thousands of years, and associating the relationships between those planets with the events that take place on Earth. This interest in astrology dates back to long before humans learned to write, so it is impossible to be precise about its exact origins. However, it is thought that the Sumerians practiced some form of astrology in 4300 BC, and this practice was continued by succeeding civilizations. Astrology was certainly part of the culture of Ancient Greece, and it is believed that the world's first astrology book was *Tetrabiblos*, which was written by Ptolemy (ca. AD 90–ca. AD 168), the Egyptian astronomer.

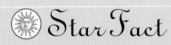

Star Fact

Until the 18th century, astrologers and astronomers could only observe the Sun, the Moon, and five planets: Mercury, Venus, Mars, Jupiter, and Saturn. Then, on March 13, 1781, the astronomer William Herschel (1738–1822) first identified the planet that became known as Uranus. Neptune was first observed by Johann Gottfried Galle (1812–1910) on the night of September 23–24, 1846, and Pluto was discovered by Clyde Tombaugh (1906–1997) on February 18, 1930.

In medieval Europe, astronomers still believed in the geocentric model of the solar system that had first been postulated by Ptolemy. He had stated that the Earth was at the center of the solar system and all the planets—including the Sun— revolved around it. However, one man disagreed. Nicolaus Copernicus (1473– 1543) was a Polish astronomer whose observations led him to conclude that the geocentric theory was completely wrong, and that all the planets, including the

THE TWELVE SIGNS OF THE ZODIAC

THE SIGNS AND THEIR PLANETS

 Aries • Mars

 Libra • Venus

 Taurus • Venus

 Scorpio • Mars/Pluto

 Gemini • Mercury

 Sagittarius • Jupiter

 Cancer • Moon

 Capricorn • Saturn

 Leo • Sun

 Aquarius • Saturn/Uranus

 Virgo • Mercury

 Pisces • Jupiter/Neptune

THE SIGNS, THEIR ELEMENTS, AND MODALITIES

	CARDINAL	FIXED	MUTABLE
FIRE	Aries	Leo	Sagittarius
EARTH	Capricorn	Taurus	Virgo
AIR	Libra	Aquarius	Gemini
WATER	Cancer	Scorpio	Pisces

THE PLANETS

Western astrology is concerned with the Sun, Moon, and the eight planets of the solar system.

The Sun

The Sun represents a person's essential self— their individuality and their essence. The sign in which the Sun is placed at the time of birth (in other words, the star sign) shows the ways in which that person needs to shine and be at their most creative. For instance, someone with the Sun in Libra expresses their true self in relationships, while a person with the Sun in Pisces does so through sensitivity and compassion. The Sun is the planetary ruler of Leo.

The Moon

The Moon is the fastest-moving planet, switching signs roughly every two and a half days. It represents a person's instinctive reactions, their habits, their moods, what feels familiar to them, and what feels safe. The Moon also describes their nurturing abilities toward themselves and others, their relationship with food, and the type of environment they like. The Moon can also represent the person's mother. The Moon is the planetary ruler of Cancer.

 Star Fact

In astrology, the Sun and Moon are referred to as planets, even though astrologers know that the Sun is a star and the Moon is the Earth's satellite.

Mercury

This tiny planet governs all forms of communication. It represents the way a person thinks and speaks, as well as what they think and speak about. Are they a skilled communicator or do they struggle to convey their ideas? Do they concentrate on practical, day-to-day matters or are they more concerned with theories and beliefs? Mercury indicates their favored methods of communication and how readily or reluctantly they connect with other people. It can also describe the person's siblings. Mercury is the planetary ruler of both Gemini and Virgo.

Venus

Venus governs our ability to enjoy ourselves and to express love. Its position in a chart shows what gives that person pleasure and the type of activities they most enjoy, how they express their affection toward others, and their particular style of showing love and consideration. Venus also describes the person's appreciation of beauty, as well as what they find beautiful. In a man's chart, Venus can describe the sort of woman he finds attractive. Venus is the planetary ruler of both Taurus and Libra.

 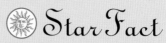

Some of the planetary rulerships changed when the three "modern" planets— Uranus, Neptune, and Pluto— were discovered. Saturn had been the sole ruler of Aquarius but Uranus was eventually regarded as the sign's modern planetary ruler. In the same way, Neptune was assigned the rulership of Pisces, previously governed by Jupiter, and Pluto was given the rulership of Scorpio, which was previously governed by Mars. Traditional astrologers still use the original rulerships.

PRINCE GEORGE'S NATAL CHART

Here is the natal chart for Prince George of Cambridge. He was born minutes before the Sun moved out of Cancer and shortly before the culmination of the Full Moon. This planetary combination indicates great emotional sensitivity, an enjoyment of family life, and a strong sense of duty and responsibility. With seven planets in cardinal signs (Uranus in Aries; Jupiter, Mars, Mercury, and the Sun in Cancer; and Pluto and the Moon in Capricorn), the prince will be highly motivated. Please see p. 180 for a key to the symbols used in this chart.

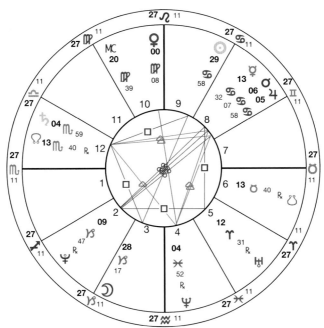

Monday, July 22, 2013 • 4:24:16 PM GMD
Paddington, England
Tropical Equal True Node

Mars

A person's desire to assert themselves, and the way in which they are able to do so, is shown by the position of Mars in their chart. Mars was the god of war, and his planetary namesake shows a person's level and style of aggression, such as the ways in which they get what they want. It also indicates how the person is able to show anger, whether this comes easily or is difficult to express. Mars is the planetary ruler of Aries and the traditional ruler of Scorpio.

Jupiter

In traditional astrology, Jupiter is known as the greater benefic because of all the good things it can bestow: it is often thought of as the planet of luck and opportunity. Jupiter rules expansion, both mental and physical. It governs further education, the acquisition of knowledge, wisdom, beliefs, and philosophies. It also rules travel, whether of the mind or the body. Jupiter is the planetary ruler of Sagittarius and the traditional ruler of Pisces.

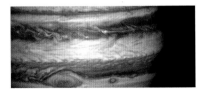

Saturn

This planet, which is traditionally called the greater malefic, is associated with limits, restrictions, delays, and rules. Although these can seem harsh areas, Saturn is the great teacher, ensuring that we learn from our experiences and gain wisdom with time, which is another area of life that Saturn governs. Saturn helps us to create structure and form, to crystallize whatever we have set out to do. Saturn is the planetary ruler of Capricorn and the traditional ruler of Aquarius.

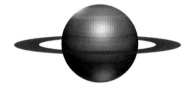

Uranus

You are never quite sure what you're going to get with Uranus. This is the planet of surprise, shock, and revolution, because Uranus likes to shake things up and turn them on their head. This planet brings a huge drive for independence and a rejection of whatever is conventional or hidebound. Uranus is the modern planetary ruler of Aquarius.

Neptune

Neptune is associated with confusion, dreams, muddles, and mysteries. It can also represent escapism, idealism, and a need to romanticize the more mundane aspects of life. Neptune is a powerfully artistic and sensitive planet, and at its best is extremely compassionate and self-sacrificing. It is the modern planetary ruler of Pisces.

 Star Fact

In 2006 the International Astronomical Association downgraded Pluto from being a planet to a dwarf planet. This may have significance to astronomers, but Pluto's demotion has made no difference to its astrological importance and power.

 Star Fact

A natal chart contains not only the person's star (or Sun) sign but also the position of the Moon, Mercury, Venus, Mars, Jupiter, Saturn, Uranus, Neptune, and Pluto at the time of their birth. An astrologer reads the natal chart by interpreting the position of each planet and their relationships to one another.

Pluto

Pluto is the planet of transformation on every level, from physical change to psychological breakthroughs. It has a powerful reputation because it rules taboos, as well as what is hidden or secret. Pluto's areas include sex, death, taxes, and anything else that is inescapable. Pluto is the modern planetary ruler of Scorpio.

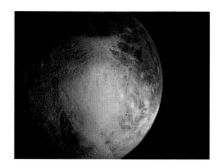

DECANATES

Each sign of the zodiac consists of 30°. Some astrologers divide each sign into three smaller segments of 10° each, called decantes. Each one is ruled by one of the three signs and planets that belong to that sign's element, beginning with the sign itself. The first decanate of each sign is ruled only by that sign and its planetary ruler. The second and third decanates are colored by the element's second and third signs respectively, and their corresponding ruling planet. For instance, someone born during the first ten days (the first decanate) of Taurus is ruled solely by Taurus and Venus. But a Taurean born between the eleventh and twentieth day is colored by Virgo, the next sign in the earth element, and its ruling planet Mercury.

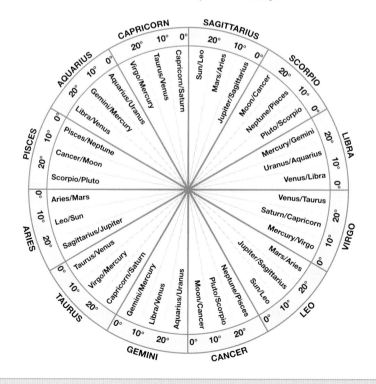

THE ARIES FILES

MARCH 21–APRIL 21

"Do not follow where the path may lead. Go instead where there is no path and leave a trail."

—Ralph Waldo Emerson

*A*ries is the first sign of the zodiac, which explains why Arians have such a strong need to be first in everything they do. They like to think of themselves as leaders, not followers. This is an impatient, ever-ready and energetic sign, whose bright, enthusiastic, and confident persona can mask a more sensitive and vulnerable interior.*

THE ARIES WOMAN

Never underestimate Ms. Aries. She may give the impression of being easygoing and mild-mannered, but if you push her too far you'll know all about it sooner or later. Here is a powerful woman who knows her own mind and isn't afraid to say what she thinks. Just like her male counterpart, Ms. Aries is competitive and highly motivated, and she frequently has her sights set on a successful career. If she has children, she will do her best to combine being a mother with continuing to work, which will help her to retain her independence and keep the sense of still being someone in her own right. Any Aries woman who feels restricted or hampered in any way will soon become extremely frustrated at not being able to achieve what she wants and will feel resentful. She may not want to be the boss in a relationship, but she certainly wants a sense of equality.

In true Aries style, Ms. Aries is an idealist and a romantic. She gets involved time and time again with the same type of partner, even if her heart is broken after each encounter. Billie Holiday's songs were especially evocative of this sort of Aries heartbreak. Generally speaking, Ms. Aries would much rather be happy because this is definitely not the sign of a martyr, and will support her partner as much as possible if she thinks they deserve it. She is forgiving and understanding, but only up to a point. She certainly won't tolerate any bad behavior for long before putting her foot down and issuing a few ground rules. The sign of Aries is renowned for its quick temper, and Ms. Aries has no compunction in shouting and stamping her feet when she think the situation demands it. Watch out for fireworks!

An Aries woman may look completely feminine and give every impression of being as sweet as sugar, but a strong core of steel runs through her. She can be direct, forthright, and blunt, and has no difficulty in asking for what she wants. Although this can be a tremendous asset whenever she needs to assert herself, especially in a male-dominated environment, it can make her seem extremely single-minded, uncompromising, and possibly even ruthless. As a result, people may be on their guard with her—an attitude that hurts and confuses her, because she usually doesn't realize how powerful she is.

THE ARIES CHILD

This child is a real live wire. They are interested in what is going on around them from an early age, and their determination to explore their surroundings in adventurous and inquisitive ways can be so devil-amay-care that they terrify their parents. As a toddler, they will scoot around the house at a spanking pace, experimenting with whatever they find. The inevitable result is plenty of bangs and bruises, leading to tears and yells. However, the child will forget about their injuries as soon as they find something else to investigate. Even as a baby, the Aries child is entertaining company, but also quite demanding, managing to get into all sorts of scrapes.

One of the most typical Arian characteristics is an element of self-centeredness. This is especially marked in Arian children because they have every reason to believe that the world revolves around them. Their parents, regardless of how much they may dote on their tiny Aries, will do their child a lifelong favor if they can teach them to be less selfish and to consider other people's needs as well as their own. Something else the parents might be able to teach the Aries child is an element of patience. This may be much easier said than done, because an Aries child finds it hard to understand the concept of having to wait for anything, especially if it involves a treat. They will lie awake all night in feverish anticipation of their birthday, Christmas, or the start of their holidays, robbing the rest of the household of their sleep too.

Star Fact

Aries is the sign of the ram. Sheep are the animals most closely associated with the early spring—the time of the year when the Sun moves through the sign of Aries.

Another Aries trait is enthusiasm about starting new ventures, and the Aries child is always beginning new projects. However, they find it much harder to keep going at the first sign of a snag or when the first flush of enthusiasm wears off. They'll be tempted to abandon whatever they have begun and start something new, and ideally should be encouraged to be a little more persistent. Again, this will stand them in good stead in later life.

The Aries child is very loving and friendly, and will lavish affection on their siblings provided that they don't present too much competition for their parents' attention. They have plenty of friends, with whom they enjoy lots of rough and tumble, preferably outdoors in the fresh air. An Aries child can only stay cooped up indoors for so long before needing to burn off all their excess energy.

APRIL 21–MAY 21

"*I never lose an opportunity of urging a practical beginning, however small, for it is wonderful how often in such matters the mustard-seed germinates and roots itself.*"

—Florence Nightingale

Taureans like to take things fairly slowly. They prefer to be unhurried and to work their way steadily through whatever they are doing without making a lot of fuss or drawing too much attention to themselves. This sign is renowned for being grounded and determined, and Taureans will devote years of effort to a project if they think it is worth their while.

HOW TO SPOT A TAURUS

Tradition states that Taureans are among the most attractive members of the zodiac. Both sexes know how to look good, taking care to choose clothes that suit them and enjoying the appearance and texture of beautiful fabrics such as wool, silk, and pure cotton. They are much happier wearing natural fibers than man-made ones, if their budget permits. If money is tight, a Taurean is clever at revamping their old clothes, perhaps by giving them a contemporary twist or by emphasizing their vintage quality. A typical Taurean likes to draw attention to their throat and neck, which is often a very elegant area of their body. They may wear scarves, clothes with distinctive collars, or necklaces and chokers. Having Venus as their planetary ruler gives Taurus their wonderful good looks, lovely skin, and often an equally lovely and sensuous figure when young. However, they become more bulky as they get older and may struggle to control their weight.

BEHIND THE SIGNS

Taurus
Vital Statistics

ELEMENT: Earth
MODALITY: Fixed
PLANETARY RULER: Venus
COLORS: Green, brown
DAY OF THE WEEK: Friday
GEMSTONE: Emerald
TOP TEN TRAITS:
Faithful • Down-to-earth •
Practical • Steady •
Deliberate • Traditional •
Sensuous • Tactile •
Possessive • Stubborn

THE TAURUS MAN

You know where you are with a Taurean man, because what you see is pretty much what you get. There are no nasty surprises and usually no hidden sides to his personality because he's too straightforward for any trickery. This is all thanks to the earth element to which he belongs, plus the fixed nature of his sign. This combination of earth and fixity makes him grounded, sure of himself, and reliable. He has dogged determination, too, which gives him the ability to work long and hard at anything he considers to be important. It's a point of honor for him to be persistent and not to give in, regardless of the odds he may be facing.

This stolid nature can sometimes spill over into the stubbornness for which the bull, the animal associated with Taurus, is so renowned. When Mr. Taurus thinks he's right and you're wrong, he'll dig in his heels and stand his ground, and if you manage to persuade him to change his mind you can pat yourself on the back for having worked a minor miracle. This tendency to be obstinate and intransigent can be a tremendous asset when Mr. Taurus needs to stick to his guns, but it can also be a stumbling block because it can make him so inflexible. You have only to look at the list of Taurean dictators to see how entrenched Taurus men can become.

Luckily for Mr. Taurus, he is ruled by Venus, the planet of love, pleasure, and beauty. Venus's influence endows him with tremendous charm and a twinkle in his eye, just like Pierce Brosnan or George Clooney. These assets certainly help to lighten his more stolid side, and they are also formidable arsenals when he wants to get his own way. Venus can also give Mr. Taurus good looks (or the sort of winning personality that makes him seem stunningly attractive) and a honeyed voice. He has a hedonistic appreciation of life's many comforts and treats, and the results of this luxury-loving side of his personality can often be seen in his heavy build. Orson Welles, who was a heavyweight in more ways than one, was a Taurean.

Venus's rulership of love makes Mr. Taurus extremely sensual and he can be highly sexed, as this is a wonderful outlet for the emotions that he feels, but may be too embarrassed to put into words. He is one of the most faithful and loyal signs of the zodiac, and expects his partner to be the same. Mr. Taurus may play the field when he's younger, but it's not long before he starts looking for a lifelong partner that he can trust and count on, just as they can rely on him.

FAMOUS TAURUS MEN

William Shakespeare • *playwright* • *April 23, 1564*
Al Pacino (above left) • *actor* • *April 25, 1940*
Michael Palin • *actor and writer* • *May 5, 1943*
Sigmund Freud • *psychoanalyst* • *May 6, 1856*
David Attenborough • *broadcaster and naturalist* • *May 8, 1926*
J. M. Barrie • *novelist and playwright* • *May 9, 1860*
Fred Astaire • *dancer and actor* • *May 10, 1899*
Salvador Dalí • *painter* • *May 11, 1904*
Stevie Wonder (above right) • *musician* • *May 13, 1950*
Liberace • *musician* • *May 16, 1919*

FAMOUS TAURUS WOMEN

Charlotte Brontë • *writer* • *April 21, 1816*
Shirley Temple Black • *actress and politician* • *April 23, 1928*
Mary Wollstonecraft • *writer and women's rights activist* • *April 27, 1759*
Audrey Hepburn (above right) • *actress* • *May 4, 1929*
Tammy Wynette • *singer* • *May 5, 1942*
Adele (above left) • *musician* • *May 5, 1988*
Eva Perón • *First Lady of Argentina* • *May 7, 1919*
Florence Nightingale • *social reformer* • *May 12, 1820*
Katharine Hepburn • *actress* • *May 12, 1907*
Margot Fonteyn • *ballerina* • *May 18, 1919*

HOW TO SPOT A GEMINI

Gemini is the Peter Pan of the zodiac. A typical Gemini usually looks younger than their true age and emphasizes this by choosing clothes that are youthful and relaxed. They particularly love wearing stripes or spots, and enjoy dressing in two colors such as blue and white. Their movements are quick and bird-like, giving them a rather elfin quality, and their lively eyes take in everything that's going on around them. They are usually slender, and retain their slim shape throughout their lives. Another telltale clue when identifying a Gemini is the way they talk with their hands and arms. This sign gesticulates a lot, often without realizing it. They like adorning their fingers with rings, and if they wear bracelets and bangles you will hear these clanking together whenever the Gemini waves their arms around. Accessories are another Gemini favorite, including bags and belts, and most self-respecting Geminis are never seen without their cell phones. They may carry a laptop or tablet around with them too, so they need never be out of contact with the rest of the world.

Gemini
Vital Statistics

ELEMENT: Air
MODALITY: Mutable
PLANETARY RULER: Mercury
COLOR: Yellow
DAY OF THE WEEK: Wednesday
GEMSTONE: Agate
TOP TEN TRAITS:
Quick-witted • Versatile • Talkative • Lively • Restless • Mercurial • Dextrous • Clever • Flirtatious • Mendacious

THE GEMINI MAN

Spending time with a Gemini man is like watching quicksilver. First he's lively, then he becomes quieter and more thoughtful. He has a restless bout of energy, then turns languid, before leaping to his feet again. He cracks jokes before effortlessly switching into a serious conversation. What's going on? Nothing. He's simply being himself. Being around Mr. Gemini for long can be a dizzying experience: here is someone who thrives on nervous energy and is easily bored, so is always looking for entertainment.

Being born under an air sign endows Mr. Gemini with a good brain, but being ruled by Mercury, the planet of communication, gives him an extra intellectual edge. Some Gemini men are formidably intelligent, with a wide range of skills, even though they do their best to hide it. Hugh Laurie's abilities as an actor, musician, and writer show what an all-rounder a Gemini can be. The mutable quality of this sign gives Mr. Gemini his adaptability and also his need not to get bogged down in anything he considers to be boring or restrictive.

And there's the rub. Mr. Gemini needs always to be kept on his toes, not only intellectually, but emotionally, too. When looking for a partner, he needs someone who is endlessly amusing and interesting, and who matches him brain cell for brain cell. Unless he has plenty of stabilizing Taurus or devoted Cancer in his chart, once the first flush of romance has gone he can develop a roving eye at best and the morals of an alley cat at worst. While many Gemini men are faithful, others enjoy the buzz that comes from infidelity. President John F. Kennedy became almost as renowned for his endless sexual conquests as for his politics.

Gemini is the trickster sign of the zodiac, and honesty isn't always at the top of Mr. Gemini's list of virtues. The Artful Dodger, who was Fagin's top pickpocket in Charles Dickens' novel *Oliver Twist*, must surely have been a Gemini. Another famous literary Gemini is Sherlock Holmes, with his ability to observe, analyze, put two and two together and always come up with the right answer.

⊛ *Star Fact*

Geminis are renowned for their duality. They are natural multitaskers and rarely do one thing at a time. It is quite typical—and natural—for a Gemini to read a magazine while watching television or holding a conversation.

FAMOUS GEMINI MEN

Bob Dylan • *singer* • *May 24, 1941*
Ralph Waldo Emerson • *writer* • *May 25, 1803*
Ian Fleming • *author* • *May 28, 1908*
Clint Eastwood • *actor and director* • *May 31, 1930*
Marquis de Sade • *writer* • *June 2, 1740*
Raoul Dufy • *painter* • *June 3, 1877*
Rafael Nadal (above right) • *tennis player* • *June 3, 1986*
John Maynard Keynes • *economist* • *June 5, 1883*
Johnny Depp (above left) • *actor* • *June 9, 1963*
Jean-Paul Sartre • *philosopher* • *June 21, 1905*

FAMOUS GEMINI WOMEN

Elizabeth Fry • *prison reformer* • *May 21, 1780*
Joan Collins • *actress* • *May 23, 1933*
Kristin Scott Thomas • *actress* • *May 24, 1960*
Marilyn Monroe • *actress* • *June 1, 1926*
Angelina Jolie (above right) • *actress* • *June 4, 1975*
Judy Garland (above left) • *singer and actress* • *June 10, 1922*
Anne Frank • *diarist* • *June 12, 1929*
Venus Williams • *tennis player* • *June 17, 1980*
Aung San Suu Kyi • *politician* • *June 19, 1945*
Nicole Kidman • *actress* • *June 20, 1967*

THE GEMINI WOMAN

There's an unpredictable quality to Ms. Gemini that you either love or hate. And she can switch from one persona to another so quickly that you may wonder if she has a twin sister that she's never told you about. This is especially true if she has several planets in Gemini, because that will make her very changeable indeed. If you enjoy being with someone whose moods switch in a millisecond and who always has something interesting to tell you, then you will love her company. But if you want a woman who is as predictable and traditional as Big Ben, you're barking up the wrong tree.

Ms. Gemini can be intensely feminine, with a gamine look that emphasizes her elfin fragility, just like Kylie Minogue. Like her male counterpart, she lives on her nerves, which can do wonders for her waistline, but makes it tricky to relax. Although she has a loving nature and enjoys having a partner in her life (provided that they have the brains to keep up with her, otherwise they quickly become history), she may not be interested in having children. Many Gemini women prefer to pursue a satisfying career than to restrict themselves, as they see it, by bringing up a family. However, Geminis can be unpredictable; the singer Josephine Baker bucked this trend by adopting twelve children of different nationalities in her "rainbow family." Those who do become mothers will expect their children to be relatively self-sufficient, such as making their own supper, because the typical Gemini mother will have so many outside interests that she won't have the time to pander to her children's every need. She's the sort of woman who, when faced with the choice between reading (or writing) a novel and washing the kitchen floor will have no problems in making up her mind. She may even be mystified by houseproud women, wondering how they can bear to do the dusting when they could be busy with something much more interesting.

Gossip and Geminis go together, and Ms. Gemini loves to know what's going on around her. At her best, she simply observes people and their fascinating idiosyncrasies, marveling at the endless quirks of human nature with her sharp wit. Razor-tongued Joan Rivers and the characters played by Joan Collins are great Gemini examples. It's the perfect inspiration for her diary, website, blog, or the stand-up comedy routine she does at weekends. But at the other end of the scale she will enjoy dishing the dirt, analyzing other people's actions in minute detail, and keeping the rumor mill turning.

THE GEMINI CHILD

The Gemini child has a natural curiosity about the world almost from the minute they are born. A Gemini baby often looks as though they have plenty to say long before they are able to speak. They seem to be bursting with ideas and observations. Their innate dexterity, which they get from their ruling planet Mercury, means that the Gemini baby enjoys watching and playing with objects from an early age, so they delight in mobiles that hang above their cot and toys that rattle or make noises. It is a rare Gemini who dislikes reading, so it is a good idea to introduce books to the child at a very early age. They respond very well to anything that stimulates their brain and gets them thinking.

 Star Fact

Gemini contains three decanates of 10° each (see p. 21). Geminis born in the first decanate have the typical Gemini alertness and need for variety. Those born in the second decanate have the charm and interest in relationships shown by their sub-rulers Libra and Venus. Those born in the third decanate have the independence and idiosyncrasy of their sub-rulers Aquarius and Uranus.

This child is a quick developer, eager to walk and talk as soon as possible and often earlier than their contemporaries. No sooner has the Gemini baby mastered crawling than they will want to be everywhere at once and will rush around getting into plenty of mischief. Thanks to their busy mind and active imagination, the Gemini child can find it difficult to go to sleep, devising lots of strategies to keep their parents fully occupied with them and always wanting one more bedtime story. Even when they do finally fall asleep they will wake up frequently, and they are often

awake and happily occupied long before the rest of the house stirs each morning.

Gemini is such a sociable sign that the Gemini child needs plenty of friends of their own age, but they will also enjoy getting to know older relatives and asking them endless questions. They love playing games, especially if these involve hide and seek, word or memory games, or dressing up. Easily bored and all too willingly distracted, the Gemini child may have to be encouraged to do their homework instead of whiling away the hours in front of a computer or television, or nattering on the phone to their friends. Although this will feel like a chore at the time, it will encourage them to strengthen their powers of concentration for later in life.

JUNE 21–JULY 22

*"Mid pleasures and palaces though we may roam,
Be it ever so humble, there's no place like home."*

—*Clari, the Maid of Milan*, J. H. Payne

C ancer is the sign of the Crab, and there are many connections between them. Crabs walk sideways and Cancerians also like to approach life from an angle rather than head-on. Cancerians are renowned for their tenacity, just like the crab's claws gripping a tasty morsel and not letting go. Cancerians are very sensitive and emotional, with a strong love for their home and family.

THE CANCER WOMAN

One of the most striking qualities of a Cancerian woman is her strong maternal streak. It may not be visible all the time but it is there, regardless of whether she has a brood of her own children or a collection of friends and family who depend on her. Ms. Cancer loves taking care of people. She enjoys cooking for them, making them tempting little treats such as rich chocolate cakes or rib-sticking suppers, to show she cares. In fact, she thinks it's rude if she doesn't have something delectably edible to offer visitors when they drop in. In an ideal world she will have made it herself but often, much to her regret, her hectic career doesn't allow that.

The cardinal quality of Cancer makes this woman very powerful and keen to succeed. One example of a highly motivated Cancerian woman is Emmeline Pankhurst, who worked so tirelessly for British women to be given the vote. Not every Cancerian woman can attain Mrs. Pankhurst's level of achievement, but even so she will work hard to get where she wants to be, and if she has a family she will do her very best to juggle her domestic and job responsibilities even though that won't always be easy. What she can't achieve, she will fret over and feel guilty about—something that is second nature to her.

Being a water sign that is ruled by the Moon makes Ms. Cancer highly emotional. She will do her best to hide this from public gaze, but her sentimentality and inner gooeyness will soon become apparent when you get to know her better and she drops her defenses. She is easily moved to tears over all sorts of things that other signs don't even notice, and has a great need to feel secure emotionally. She has tremendous intuition and imagination too, which can be very helpful and steer her in the right direction, but can also make her imagine the worst for absolutely no good reason. At times Ms. Cancer can become moody and over-emotional, so the people near her feel as though they're tiptoeing around her. Her protective nature makes her want to spring to the aid of anyone who is suffering, and some Cancerian women, including Diana, Princess of Wales, and Esther Rantzen, have made this a personal crusade.

THE CANCER CHILD

One thing is certain with a Cancerian child. Regardless of where in the world they are born and the culture in which they grow up, one person will dominate and color their life: their mother. She will have a very strong influence on the child, whether for good or ill, and the little Cancerian will endure tremendous separation anxiety whenever their mother isn't around. As a result, persuading a Cancerian child to go to nursery school can be quite a struggle, as there will be fountains of tears and yells of protest at the thought of having to leave the comfort of home and mother, even for a few hours a day. The parents need to devise some clever strategies to encourage their child to venture happily out into the wider world and not look on it as something to be feared.

 Star Fact

When the celebrated Greek hero Heracles battled with the Hydra, a monstrous many-headed serpent, a giant crab pinched Heracles's foot. Heracles killed the crab by treading on it. The goddess Hera was so delighted with the crab's defense of the Hydra that she placed it in the heavens, in the constellation of Cancer.

FAMOUS LEO MEN

Benito Mussolini • *politician* • *July 29, 1883*
Yves Saint Laurent • *couturier* • *August 1, 1936*
Barack Obama (above right) • *politician* • *August 4, 1961*
Neil Armstrong • *astronaut* • *August 5, 1930*
Sir Alexander Fleming • *bacteriologist* • *August 6, 1881*
Dustin Hoffman • *actor* • *August 8, 1937*
Alfred Hitchcock (above left) • *film director* • *August 13, 1899*
Fidel Castro • *politician* • *August 13, 1926*
Napoleon I • *emperor* • *August 15, 1769*
Robert de Niro • *actor* • *August 17, 1943*

FAMOUS LEO WOMEN

Rose Kennedy • *matriarch* • *July 22, 1890*
Amelia Earhart • *aviator* • *July 24, 1897*
Jacqueline Kennedy Onassis • *First Lady* • *July 28, 1929*
Emily Brontë • *writer* • *July 30, 1818*
Kate Bush • *singer* • *July 30, 1958*
Her Majesty The Queen Mother • *monarch* • *August 4, 1900*
Mata Hari • *spy* • *August 7, 1876*
Melanie Griffith (above right) • *actress* • *August 9, 1957*
Whitney Houston (above left) • *singer* • *August 9, 1963*
Julia Child • *chef and TV personality* • *August 15, 1912*

HOW TO SPOT A VIRGO

Even when they are in their oldest clothes there is an element of neatness to a Virgo. It is as if they couldn't look truly messy even if they tried. Generally speaking, a Virgo hates to think that they look untidy because then they feel uncomfortable, so they prefer to make an effort with their appearance. They look good in slightly formal, tailored clothes that show off their slim figure, and have a particular affinity for shades of navy, brown and gray. They like to brighten up this sophisticated palette with polka dots, small checks and tiny floral patterns, although putting together too many of these can look bitty. Being ruled by Mercury means that Virgos have a naturally slim build, like their Gemini cousins, and unless their lives are very sedentary they are unlikely to have many weight problems. They look intelligent and quick-witted, with darting eyes that don't miss anything. Their hair tends to be of medium thickness and texture, with a widow's peak, but the men often lose their hair at an early age.

Virgo Vital Statistics

ELEMENT: Earth
MODALITY: Mutable
PLANETARY RULER: Mercury
COLORS: Green, brown, navy blue
DAY OF THE WEEK: Wednesday
GEMSTONE: Sardonyx
TOP TEN TRAITS: Modest • Perfectionist • Analytical • Reliable • Methodical • Shy • Anxious • Industrious • Critical • Pedantic

THE VIRGO MAN

There is something very black and white about this man. He exudes a practical, no-nonsense attitude that suggests he knows what's what and he doesn't like being mucked about. Some signs run a mile from a crisis but a Virgo man thrives when the chips are down, because it means he can get busy with one of his favorite occupations—rolling up his sleeves and creating order out of chaos. He may also throw in a few words of advice about not letting the problem happen again, and will follow these up with some criticism, just in case you didn't get the message. Sometimes Mr. Virgo really lets rip, at which point he can become overcritical and won't know when to stop.

It isn't only Mr. Virgo's personality that is very black and white. His clothes tend to be as well, because he likes to look smart, respectable, and well turned out. Put a typical Virgo man in a hectically patterned shirt and he's in danger of passing out from embarrassment, although some Virgos, such as Freddie Mercury, prefer to create a wildly flamboyant image that reveals an entirely different side to this modest earth sign. The fictional detective Hercule Poirot, with his fastidious and pernickety ways, can only have been a Virgo. Luckily, most male Virgos don't take things to such extremes.

Being ruled by communicative Mercury makes Mr. Virgo intelligent and analytical. He loves to chew over problems, find the patterns within them and work out solutions. He's in love with words, too, so it's no surprise that it was a Virgo—Dr. Samuel Johnson—who compiled the first English-language dictionary. Mercury also makes him light on his feet like dancer Gene Kelly, and clever with his hands like the magician David Copperfield. This planet loves dealing with ideas, but isn't so comfortable when it comes to expressing emotions, so Mr. Virgo can become completely tongue-tied in romantic situations. It isn't that he can't feel love and emotion, it's simply that he doesn't quite know how to handle them because they are messy and unpredictable.

He isn't the most paternal sign of the zodiac either, and many male Virgos are quite happy not to have children. If they do come along, he will struggle to cope with the trail of devastation they leave behind them, and must guard against being too strict or domineering with them in his anxiety about bringing them up properly. If he can relax and remember that childhood is meant to be fun—even if his own was rather tense or dutiful—he will have taken the first step in learning to be a more easygoing father.

 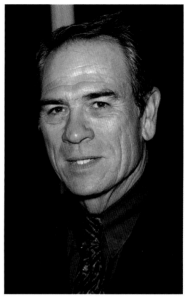

FAMOUS VIRGO MEN

Stephen Fry • *actor and writer* • *August 24, 1957*
Michael Jackson • *singer* • *August 29, 1958*
Van Morrison • *singer* • *August 31, 1945*
Keanu Reeves (above left) • *actor* • *September 2, 1964*
Leo Tolstoy • *writer* • *September 9, 1828*
Otis Redding • *singer* • *September 9, 1941*
Tommy Lee Jones (above right) • *actor* • *September 15, 1946*
Lance Armstrong • *cyclist* • *September 18, 1971*
Stephen King • *writer* • *September 21, 1947*
David Copperfield • *illusionist* • *September 16, 1956*

FAMOUS VIRGO WOMEN

Claudia Schiffer • *model* • *August 25, 1970*
Mother Teresa (above left) • *nun* • *August 26, 1910*
Cameron Diaz • *actress* • *August 30, 1972*
Beyoncé (above right) • *singer* • *September 4, 1981*
Raquel Welch • *actress* • *September 5, 1940*
Agatha Christie • *writer* • *September 15, 1890*
Lauren Bacall • *actress* • *September 16, 1924*
Greta Garbo • *actress* • *September 18, 1905*
Twiggy • *model* • *September 19, 1949*
Sophia Loren • *actress* • *September 20, 1934*

THE VIRGO WOMAN

You need to be on your best behavior when you first meet a female Virgo. Even though she will be too polite to make it obvious that she's watching you, you can bet that she'll notice if you eat in ways that would make a pig blush, are lacking in manners, or scoff all the potatoes. And not only will she notice but she may decide to give you only one more chance before quietly edging you out of her life. This doesn't mean she can't have fun because, like the writer Dorothy Parker, she's witty, quick-thinking, and terrific company. She may look neat and tidy, with shining hair and immaculately pressed clothes, but she's much more complicated at heart. She can also feel constrained by her perfect image, feeling that it gives a false impression of who she really is. The actress Ingrid Bergman, with her cool beauty, was considered to be the ideal woman until she caused a huge scandal by leaving her husband for another man.

When Ms. Virgo is frazzled and worried, she has a tendency to give herself a very hard time. She will criticize herself, whether or not it's justified, endlessly replay what she believes to be her mistakes, and have sleepless nights fretting about it all. The self-imposed anxiety can affect her stomach and play havoc with her digestion, giving this modest woman yet another reason to feel self-conscious, nervous, and embarrassed. If she has a deadline or a duty, she will meticulously work away at it, even if she never quite meets her own high standards. She will also do her very best if she becomes a mother, even though Virgo itself isn't a very maternal sign. Despite loving her children, she will struggle to cope with the mess and noise that they create, and she will also crave some intellectual stimulus if she's a stay-at-home mother.

The combination of being born into a mutable earth sign and being ruled by Mercury gives this woman a brain. She's smart and intelligent, and she's quickly frustrated if she isn't given the chance to put her skills to the test. Sometimes, her sharp mental faculties can make less brainy people uncomfortable, at which point she is quite likely to play down her abilities in case she gives the impression of being egotistical or too big for her boots—two character traits that make her shudder with horror. Yet, given her innate modesty, she is unlikely to ever be guilty of either of them.

THE VIRGO CHILD

Many children need to be encouraged to take responsibility and to develop their practical skills, rather than to spend all their time playing. The Virgo child, on the other hand, may have to be encouraged to relax a little and not be so focused on what they think they ought to be doing. They may even have to be shooed out into the garden, away from their books or computer, so they can relax and get some fresh air. The fact is that the Virgo child has a strong sense of duty, which usually serves them well, but can sometimes make life a serious business for them.

It's essential for a Virgo child to be encouraged to use their brain in whichever way suits them best. Virgo rules small things and a Virgo child is

Star Fact

Virgo has three decanates of 10° each (see p. 21). Virgos born in the first decanate have the characteristic Virgo perfectionism and nervous energy. Those born in the second decanate are sub-ruled by Capricorn and Saturn, making them hard-working and grounded. Those born in the third decanate are practical and pleasure-loving, courtesy of their sub-rulers Taurus and Venus.

often fascinated by what they can see under a microscope—the discovery of what is usually an invisible world engrosses them and can spark off a lifelong thirst for knowledge. Being an earth sign means they benefit from being surrounded by nature, not only because they are literally in their element but because rolling around, jumping in puddles, and getting their clothes in a state does them the world of good. The Virgo tendency to worry and agonize over tiny details starts at an early age, so the Virgo child needs to learn how to deal with this anxious side of their personality. Their enquiring mind will prompt them to ask their parents all sorts of questions, often about tricky topics, and they will know if they're being fobbed off with easy answers. Ideally, they should be treated with honesty, and also encouraged to think

for themselves. If their worries keep them awake at night, it will be far better to discuss what's bothering them in a constructive way than to make light of their fears or, worst of all, ridicule them.

One classic Virgo character trait is shyness, so the Virgo child should be gently encouraged to mix with other children rather than to spend too much time by themselves. They will be much happier if they have siblings or friends they can rely on, and who will coax them out of their shell. Don't expect a Virgo child to be overly affectionate because it's not in their character unless they have plenty of Leo or Libra in their chart. You will have to encourage them to become more demonstrative and to talk about their feelings, so they feel better able to open up and let their emotions flow in a healthy way.

SEPTEMBER 22-OCTOBER 23

"We love being in love, that's the truth on't."

—*Henry Esmond*, W. M. Thackeray

*L*ibrans are renowned for their charm, refinement, and ability to get on well with almost everyone. They are the diplomats of the zodiac, with a deep need to create and maintain harmonious relationships, and many of them would rather be in a challenging relationship than on their own. One classic Libran characteristic is indecisiveness, which can lead to much dithering and anxiety.

THE LIBRA WOMAN

She's one of the most feminine signs of the zodiac, thanks to her ruling planet Venus and her desire to spread sweetness and light in all directions. You have only to look at some Libran women, such as Gwyneth Paltrow and Julie Andrews, to see how Venus can endow them with a wholesome, sweet and gentle persona. Some of them look like china dolls, so fluffy, delicate, and fragile that a puff of wind would blow them over. And while some of them are certainly like that, you shouldn't be fooled. There is another side to Ms. Libra. When going after what she wants, Ms. Libra is the classic example of the iron hand in the velvet glove. The combination of her Venusian charm, intellect from her air element, and determination from her cardinality give her formidable talents. She can be much braver, more decisive, and more direct than her male counterpart, and is quite prepared to use her feminine charms as one of the weapons in her arsenal, as Margaret Thatcher so ably proved. Brigitte Bardot made her name as a sex symbol before becoming an outspoken and controversial champion of animal rights and much else besides.

In true Libran style, Ms. Libra needs a partner, or at least to be part of a team, both professionally and personally. She isn't happy going it alone, and her romantic soul is always looking for true love. If motherhood appeals, no matter how much she loves her children she will need plenty of intellectual outlets, especially if she's a full-time mother. This is a woman who loves exercising her brain and who needs plenty of opportunities to do so. Never underestimate her, because there is a l ot more to her than meets the eye. Yet she is very sensitive, even if she does her best not to show it, and her feelings are easily hurt.

Libra is the sign of the scales, which indicates the Libran need for balance. Ms. Libra certainly likes to have everything on an even keel if possible, but if life is too uneventful for too long she will manage to stir things up, even if she's not aware of doing so. Just like Mr. Libra, she can be moody and changeable, and sometimes she's difficult to please. It's often because she's feeling unappreciated, so get ready with some heartfelt compliments. She always tries to win others round with flattery and charm, so make sure she gets as good as she gives in the nicest possible way.

THE LIBRA CHILD

Even as a baby, the Libran child is a charmer. They are cuddly, affectionate, they smile winningly at all the right people, and they may even manage to produce a couple of photogenic dimples whenever a camera points in their direction. What is more, they are likely to sleep blissfully for hours on end, much to their parents' delight and relief. They get on well with their siblings, with an instinctive sense of fair play, and will be happy to share their toys without being asked. So far so good, and if there were a best-behaved baby competition they'd definitely be one of the favorites to win.

However, there are a few drawbacks. One of them is food. Librans love their food, even when they've just been weaned and are discovering the delights of mashed-up rusks garnished with squished banana. It's all too easy for a little Libran to love their food so much that they carry on eating it long after they should have stopped, with the result that they start to

The sign of Libra has three decanates of 10° each (see p. 21). Librans born in the first one have the typical Libran charm and need for relationships. Aquarius and Uranus are the sub-rulers of the second decanate, conferring a more independent and dispassionate attitude. Librans born in the third decanate enjoy variety and travel, thanks to their sub-rulers Gemini and Mercury.

gain weight, and what was once a sweetly chubby child becomes bigger and bigger. While some children might lose this weight once they become active toddlers, it can stubbornly stick around for a Libran child and may even set the tone for the future. Most Libran children have a very sweet tooth, and gifts of sweets, chocolate, and ice cream, no matter how kindly intended, will only make matters worse.

Exercise can be another tricky area for a Libran child, because very often they aren't interested in it in the slightest. They would rather play gently with their

friends or watch television, so they must be encouraged to dash around and be active. As this is such a sociable sign, one of the best ways for a Libran child to get some exercise is in the company of their friends or family, so the whole thing becomes a pleasure rather than a duty. And speaking of being sociable, a typical Libran child will soon develop a busy social life. They'll exercise their diplomatic skills by intervening when their friends fall out with one another and smoothing over any spats. They may also surprise you with their ability to see both sides of an argument—one of the greatest Libran qualities, and definitely a characteristic that will stand them in good stead throughout their lives.

THE SCORPIO FILES

OCTOBER 23–NOVEMBER 22

"Where force is necessary, one should make use of it boldly, resolutely, and right to the end. But it is as well to know the limitations of force."

—"Was Nun?" Leon Trotsky

Scorpio is the most powerful, enigmatic and intense sign of the zodiac. Like an iceberg, there is a lot going on under the surface of a Scorpio, but they will do their best to keep much of themselves and their inner workings hidden from view. As far as this very secretive and private sign is concerned, it's safer that way.

HOW TO SPOT A SCORPIO

Scorpios like to make an impact, but they do it in an idiosyncratic and rather enigmatic way. At times they come across as forceful and powerful, liking to be noticed and wearing clothes that are designed to attract attention, and on other occasions they prefer to keep a low profile, almost as though they can see you but you can't see them, and may even wear a pair of sunglasses as protection from the world. A Scorpio will dress to impress, often with rather formal outfits and beautifully tailored suits, and particularly likes clothes in black and burgundy. They can look very good in leather or suede, too. Most Scorpios have black or dark brown hair and their eyes are very noticeable, often with a piercing gaze. It is as though they can see straight through all the artifice to the real you, which can be a disconcerting experience. Scorpio women are svelte in youth but can gain weight in later years, and Scorpio men are typically stocky and muscular.

Scorpio Vital Statistics

ELEMENT: Water
MODALITY: Fixed
PLANETARY RULER: Pluto
COLORS: Dark reds
DAY OF THE WEEK: Tuesday
GEMSTONE: Opal
TOP TEN TRAITS: Faithful •
Strong-willed • Controlled •
Dramatic • Compulsive •
Powerful • Intense • Jealous •
Suspicious • Manipulative

THE SCORPIO MAN

Mr. Scorpio is a very cool customer. He knows what he wants, he knows how to get it, and he also knows how to disguise his intentions so he can keep them hidden from the rest of the world. This man likes to play his cards close to his chest, partly because he has a limited amount of trust in other people and firsthand knowledge of how treacherous they can sometimes be, and partly because life is so much easier if he can do things in the way he wants and release information on a strictly need-to-know basis. It saves so much trouble and argument!

Emotions go very deep in a Scorpio man. You can thank his water sign and his ruling planet Pluto for that. He feels things with great intensity, but you may have to wait for hell to freeze over before he opens up and confides in you about what exactly it is that he's feeling. After all, he is the most private man in the zodiac, and also one of the most self-contained, so you can take it as a tremendous compliment if he ever spills the beans to you about his innermost emotions. Generally speaking, he is much happier keeping them a secret. Yet it is essential for him to find some constructive outlets for his feelings, otherwise those years of bottled-up emotional turbulence can wreak havoc. Actually, they can cause problems even when Mr. Scorpio makes the most of his water element's creativity—Dylan Thomas, Richard Burton and Evelyn Waugh all struggled with their inner demons.

Regardless of what he does for a living, Mr. Scorpio exudes power. He needs to be in control in some way, even if he's a lowly employee. He needs to be the boss in his family too, with a tendency to lay down the law even if it's done for the very best motives. What he must guard against is letting this desire for control turn into an obsessive need to call the shots and be the king pin, because that can lead to very ruthless behavior. Like their opposite number, Taurus, some Scorpio men can become so in love with power, not to mention the conviction that they have the right to tell others what to do, that it completely affects their lives and those of the people around them. The list of such men is long, and includes Joseph Goebbels, Oswald Mosley, and Leon Trotsky. Of course, most Scorpio men never take things to such extremes, but they still need to know that they're the ones who wear the trousers, especially at home.

FAMOUS SCORPIO MEN

Bill Gates • *business magnate* • October 28, 1955
John Keats • *poet* • October 31, 1795
L. S. Lowry • *painter* • November 1, 1887
David Schwimmer • *actor* • November 2, 1966
Albert Camus • *philosopher* • November 7, 1913
George Patton • *military leader* • November 11, 1885
Leonardo DiCaprio (above right) • *actor* • November 11, 1974
Robert Louis Stevenson • *writer* • November 13, 1850
Jawaharlal Nehru • *statesman* • November 14, 1889
Martin Scorsese (above left) • *film director* • November 17, 1942

FAMOUS SCORPIO WOMEN

Julia Roberts (above left) • *actress* • October 28, 1967
Marie Antoinette (above right) • *queen consort* • November 2, 1755
Bonnie Raitt • *singer* • November 8, 1949
Demi Moore • *actress* • November 11, 1962
Whoopi Goldberg • *actress* • November 13, 1955
Margaret Atwood • *writer* • November 18, 1939
Meg Ryan • *actress* • November 19, 1961
Jodie Foster • *actress* • November 19, 1962
Goldie Hawn • *actress* • November 21, 1945
Jamie Lee Curtis • *actress* • November 22, 1958

HOW TO SPOT A SAGITTARIUS

Sagittarius is sometimes described as the eternal student, and many Sagittarians certainly like to maintain this casual and relaxed image throughout their lives. They prefer jeans to suits, for instance, or wear floaty, ethnic clothes with a distinct sixties influence. The fact is that Sagittarians are independent and love their freedom, so they aren't interested in clothes that constrain or limit them in any way. They prefer easy-care clothes, such as sweaters they can sling round their shoulders and shirts that don't need immaculate ironing. Favorite colors include purple and turquoise, and they love sophisticated patterns such as paisley. If they do have to get dressed up, they are quite likely to change back into something more comfortable at the first available moment. The typical Sagittarian is tall, with a lean, rangy body, long legs and a loping stride. Their hair has reddish highlights and they often have wide, generous mouths, with a ready smile.

BEHIND THE SIGNS

Sagittarius
Vital Statistics

ELEMENT: Fire
MODALITY: Mutable
PLANETARY RULER: Jupiter
COLOR: Purple
DAY OF THE WEEK: Thursday
GEMSTONE: Turquoise
TOP TEN TRAITS: Optimistic
• **Good-humored** • **Generous**
• **Exuberant** • **Open-minded**
• **Philosophical** • **Sagacious** •
Blunt • **Honest** • **Overblown**

THE SAGITTARIUS MAN

Life is never dull when a Sagittarian man is around. He won't let things get boring, and his antics are often designed to raise a smile at the very least, if not a full-blown belly laugh. In fact, he's one of the liveliest signs of the zodiac, thanks to the winning combination of his fire element, his ruling planet Jupiter, and his mutable quality. Fire gives him his eagerness and never-ending enthusiasm, not to mention his ability to bounce back from problems like one of those self-righting children's toys. Jupiter, the gas giant that is the biggest planet in our solar system, gives him his expansiveness, self-belief and good humor, and his mutability makes him changeable and interested in many different ideas and activities. Put all those ingredients together and you have the recipe for someone who can be larger than life.

Mr. Sagittarius can also have a high opinion of himself, and if it's allowed full rein he can become rather grandiose, with a tendency to exaggerate his exploits and overdo things. Happily, his infectious sense of humor usually catches up with him and helps him to see the funny side of his behavior. Laughter is never far away with a Sagittarian man. Some members of this sign, such as the clown Joseph Grimaldi and stand-up comedians Richard Pryor and Billy Connolly, have made a career out of their sense of humor. Others who have combined humor with writing, which is another Sagittarian talent, include Woody Allen, Bill Bryson, Mark Twain, Jonathan Swift, and Noël Coward.

Optimism is a classic Sagittarian characteristic, and Mr. Sagittarius's glass is almost always half-full. He may take the odd nosedive into doom and gloom, but he soon resurfaces because he believes that life is worth enjoying. Mr. Sagittarius does his best to make the most of every day. How does he manage this? It's simple. He loves a challenge. It can be minor or major, but he revels in setting his sights on something that he can achieve, and he's especially motivated if he's chosen what seems like mission impossible to everyone else. After all, his sign is represented by a centaur aiming an arrow at the far horizon. If it fails to hit the mark, Mr. Sagittarius will simply try again—and again—until he finally feels he's getting somewhere. Of course, there is always the chance that he won't complete his ambition because he'll be sidetracked by a different enthusiasm that springs up out of the blue and grabs his imagination. Never mind, he'll think. It's all good experience and it will certainly give him something interesting to talk about next time he holds court.

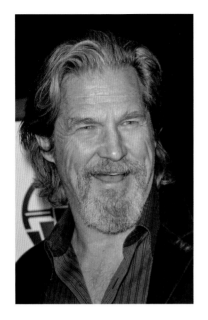

FAMOUS SAGITTARIUS MEN

Henri de Toulouse-Lautrec • *painter* • *November 24, 1864*
Jimi Hendrix • *musician* • *November 27, 1942*
Winston Churchill (above right) • *statesman* • *November 30, 1874*
Jeff Bridges (above left) • *actor* • *December 4, 1949*
Walt Disney • *film mogul* • *December 5, 1901*
Frank Sinatra • *singer* • *December 12, 1915*
Bill Nighy • *actor* • *December 12, 1949*
HH Pope Francis I • *religious leader* • *December 17, 1936*
Keith Richards • *musician* • *December 18, 1943*
Uri Geller • *psychic* • *December 20, 1946*

FAMOUS SAGITTARIUS WOMEN

Scarlett Johansson • *actress* • *November 22, 1984*
Tina Turner • *singer* • *November 26, 1939*
Louisa May Alcott • *writer* • *November 29, 1832*
Marie Tussaud • *waxwork exhibitor* • *December 1, 1761*
Maria Callas • *soprano* • *December 3, 1923*
Christina Rossetti • *poet* • *December 5, 1830*
Judi Dench (above left) • *actress* • *December 9, 1934*
Miranda Hart • *comedian* • *December 14, 1972*
Jane Austen (above right) • *writer* • *December 16, 1775*
Edith Piaf • *singer* • *December 19, 1915*

THE SAGITTARIUS WOMAN

There is often a tomboyish quality to Ms. Sagittarius. Although she may love getting dressed up in ultra-feminine outfits every now and then, at heart she's happiest in her most comfortable clothes and with the wind blowing through her hair. She may even be a bit of a tomboy throughout her life, welcoming the chance to climb trees or mess about in boats whether she's six or sixty.

In true Sagittarian style, she seeks freedom and independence, and that includes being free to do and say what she likes, when she likes. However, her tendency to say the first thing that comes into her head can test the thickness of the skin of whoever is on the receiving end of her impulsive words, because Ms. Sagittarius prides herself on her honesty. This can result in anything from an endearing foot-in-mouth syndrome to the sort of ferocious bluntness that causes cringing all round. Ms. Sagittarius will apologize and laugh it off, but deep down she won't understand what the fuss was about. After all, she'll remind herself, she was telling the truth, and what's wrong with that? Her reverence for words often spills over into a strong writing ability, in which case she follows in the footsteps of such Sagittarian women as Nancy Mitford, Willa Cather, and Frances Hodgson Burnett.

Sagittarians of both sexes like to rush into situations, and this gives Ms. Sagittarius a tendency to be accident-prone. It's not because of a lack of grace so much as her impatience to get on with things, and this hastiness can result in anything from chipped crockery to the odd bruise, but she won't mind because she's used to it. Other people may prefer that she doesn't help with the washing up, in case of breakages.

Her approach to domesticity can be equally hit and miss. At times, she delights in doing lots of cooking and cleaning, but these house-proud phases rarely last long before boredom kicks in, so the rest of the family has to learn to fend for themselves. As Ms. Sagittarius will remind them as she breezes out of the door, she has more interesting things to do with her life than the dusting. Her fire element gives her warmth and affection, but she isn't overly maternal and may think seriously about what she sees as the sacrifices that motherhood entails. If she does have children, she'll adore telling them exciting stories and encouraging them to explore the world. Her greatest gift will be to instill in them some of her own sense of adventure, independence, and thirst for knowledge, as well as her love of reading.

THE SAGITTARIUS CHILD

It's a joy to watch a Sagittarian child in action. They make full use of their imagination, they throw themselves (sometimes literally) into whatever they are doing, and they quickly bounce back from disappointment. Their exuberance can know no bounds and they never want the fun to stop, making it difficult for their exhausted parents to persuade them to go to bed at the end of another action-packed day. Here is a child who thrives on being active and burning up their seemingly endless reserves of energy. They love the rough and tumble of the school playground, they enjoy going for long meandering walks, and they revel in endless childhood adventures and scrapes. No wonder they are so popular with their friends. Yet this is a child who can have the best of both worlds,

because they adore using their brain in more intellectual pursuits, too. A small Sagittarian will already have amassed lots of different interests, some of which will

Star Fact

The constellation of Sagittarius is represented by Chiron, who was the most celebrated centaur (half man, half horse) of Greek mythology. He was wise, kind, and a great healer, and Zeus commemorated him by putting him in the heavens.

remain with them for life, and will need little encouragement to chat about them. Put the child in front of a computer and they will soon be looking up fascinating facts with which they can regale the rest of the family, as well as collecting a string of sometimes embarrassing questions to ask their parents. When they're not online, they'll love curling up with a book or possibly even writing their own. These are all indications of the trademark Sagittarian curiosity, thirst for knowledge, and craving for intellectual freedom, and any parent worth their salt will encourage their Sagittarian child to use their brain as much as possible. This child has tremendous potential, with the winning combination of versatility and intellect. They should be encouraged to seize

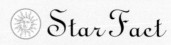

Star Fact

Sagittarius is the sign associated with luck, thanks to its ruling planet Jupiter. Jupiter brings Sagittarians many opportunities in life, both big and small, and helps them to attract good fortune by imbuing them with a positive and optimistic attitude.

opportunities, to make things happen, and to play to their strengths as well as work on their weaknesses.

Another classic Sagittarian characteristic is a tendency to see life from a philosophical viewpoint, and this also begins at an early age. Just like their opposite number Gemini, one of the favorite questions of the Sagittarian child is "Why?" and they will expect the adults around them to give sensible answers rather than to fob them off with excuses or comments about them being too young to understand. This philosophical bent may draw the child toward religion or spirituality, too, with an interest in different belief systems. It's all part of their innate need to understand the world around them.

THE CAPRICORN FILES

DECEMBER 21–JANUARY 20

*"Pessimism, when you get used to it,
is just as agreeable as optimism."*

–*Things That Have Interested Me*, Arnold Bennett

A curious thing about Capricorns is that they seem much older than their years when they're young, and much younger than their years when they're older. Life can often be tough for them at first, and it's not helped by what can be a strong tendency to look on the gloomy side, but it does get easier. With age comes experience, wisdom and a wonderfully dry sense of humor.

THE CAPRICORN WOMAN

Meet one of the most capable women in the zodiac. Ms. Capricorn knows exactly what she's doing, and probably what you are supposed to be doing, too. She likes to be organized and practical, and prides herself on her reliability, especially at work where she will slog away from dawn till dusk if necessary. It may still be a man's world, but Ms. Capricorn is determined to make her mark—and on level pegging, too. Even if she has a home and family to look after she won't want any concessions to be made on that score, and expects everyone at home to fend for themselves as best they can if she isn't around.

No wonder motherhood can be a difficult proposition for Ms. Capricorn, because it stands a good chance of interfering with her ambitions, so maintaining a happy balance between work and home can be a very difficult juggling act. She will be the best mother she can possibly be, because after all, this isn't a woman who likes to do things by halves, but sometimes she might find motherhood easier if she simply relaxed a little and stopped trying to teach her children valuable skills at every opportunity. Life isn't only about learning lessons.

Her strong sense of responsibility and the motivation that guides her each day, courtesy of her cardinal quality, can make Ms. Capricorn come across as slightly formidable. She seems so capable, so driven, and apparently incapable of suffering fools gladly. Yet that is only part of the story of this complicated woman. Despite her tough persona, she is so eager to do the right thing in order to earn other people's respect that she often allows herself to be manipulated into situations that aren't of her choosing. This is especially likely to happen before she reaches her late twenties, because at this stage in her life she's at her most impressionable and anxious. Once she's in her thirties, she begins to blossom and gains a much stronger sense of self. She also gives the impression that she's a force to be reckoned with, yet her innate vulnerability is still there if you take the trouble to look for it. She may try to hide it, but it will be painfully obvious at times. You have only to look at the cool persona of Marlene Dietrich, and the way Simone de Beauvoir held her own in French literary circles despite many emotional setbacks, to see what a powerful proposition a Capricorn woman can be.

THE CAPRICORN CHILD

Most children have to be persuaded to do their homework, tidy their rooms, and behave themselves. Capricorn children have such a strong sense of responsibility, and such a deep need to gain the respect of others by being conscientious, that they may have to be coaxed into having fun and relaxing. Enjoying themselves doesn't always come naturally, yet it's essential for the overall health of the Capricorn child. If they are the eldest child, it will be second nature for them to take care of their younger siblings, whether looking after them until their parents return home from work each day or helping them with their homework. They may struggle with their own homework, too, because while some Capricorn children are almost astonishingly brainy, others tend to develop slowly, despite all their efforts to succeed. They need encouragement and understanding, with plenty of rewards whenever they do well, but also consolation and kindness when they don't.

Their ruling planet Saturn makes the Capricorn child very conscious of their emotional security—or lack of it. They need to know that they are loved for themselves, regardless of their exam results or the state of their fingernails, and they also need to be able to talk to other people about their many worries.

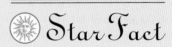 Star Fact

When Zeus was involved in a massive battle with the monster Typhon, he was helped by Aegipan, or possibly the god Pan, who was part-goat, and emerged victorious. He was so grateful, he immortalized Aegipan by setting him in the constellation of Capricorn.

Star Fact

Capricorn believes in creating things that are built to last. Perhaps surprisingly for what is considered to be such a conventional sign, quite a few inventors have been Capricorns. They include Louis Braille (January 4, 1809), who invented the eponymous system of reading for the blind; Isaac Pitman (January 4, 1813), who developed what is now the world's most popular system of shorthand; Jacques-Etienne Montgolfier (January 6, 1745) who, with his brother, invented the hot air balloon; Richard Arkwright (December 23, 1732), whose entrepreneurial skills helped to create the modern factory system; and James Watt (January 19, 1736), whose work to improve the steam engine was a major contribution to the Industrial Revolution.

The classic Capricorn tendency to be anxious starts early, so it's essential that the child can confide in at least one adult who understands their worries, and who can set their mind at rest or at least put their concerns into perspective. Without these outlets, the child may have sleepless nights, become troubled, or not do well at school.

Capricorns have a tendency to be shy and withdrawn, and the Capricorn child is no exception. Making friends, especially when they go to a new school or if they move to a new neighborhood, can be difficult for them. They may lack the confidence to chat with people they don't know, and will hang back rather than put themselves forward. This can make them seem reserved and self-contained, and possibly even aloof and distant, but once they make some good friends they will be able to relax and bring out the more lively and entertaining sides of their character.

THE AQUARIUS FILES

JANUARY 20–FEBRUARY 18

"Unless one is a genius, it is best to aim at being intelligible."

—*The Dolly Dialogues,* Anthony Hope

Aquarius is the sign that marches to a different drummer. Some Aquarians are more influenced by the sign's traditional ruler, Saturn, while others are more like its modern ruler, Uranus. Aquarians are noted for their humanitarian impulses, their egalitarian beliefs, and their innate friendliness. They can find it easier to deal with groups of people than with one-to-one relationships, which can puzzle them.

HOW TO SPOT AN AQUARIUS

Although Aquarius has a reputation for looking eccentric and striking, in reality it is the Uranian-ruled Aquarians who stand out from the crowd in this way. They like to wear highly individual clothes, following their own idiosyncratic style, and don't give two hoots if other people think them odd. Such an attitude makes little sense to Aquarians who are strongly Saturnian, because they are much more conscious of what other people think of them. Despite this, they will still enjoy creating their own look, from their hair right down to their shoes. Usually, a Uranian-influenced Aquarian likes to break the sartorial rules when they are young, taking pleasure in raising eyebrows, but they become more conventional as they get older. This may not be because they have mellowed, but simply because they were in the vanguard of the latest fashion and now everyone is copying them. Aquarians have intelligent, lively faces, and frequently have slightly crooked teeth. Favorite colors include bright blues.

Aquarius Vital Statistics

ELEMENT: Air
MODALITY: Fixed
PLANETARY RULER: Uranus
COLOR: Ultramarine
DAY OF THE WEEK: Saturday
GEMSTONE: Aquamarine
TOP TEN TRAITS: Friendly •
Unconventional • Independent •
Detached • Intelligent •
Humanitarian • Rational •
Objective • Quirky • Intractable

THE AQUARIUS MAN

You can never be quite sure what you're going to get with an Aquarius man. Sometimes he's gentle, sweet, and understanding, and at others he's rigidly rational, emotionally detached to the point of being frostier than the North Pole, and clearly of the opinion that you've lost your marbles. It's all because of the contrary nature of this most contrary of signs. If there's one rule to remember above all others for Mr. Aquarius it is to expect the unexpected, because you never know what he will say or do next. He has his modern planetary ruler, Uranus, to thank for this, because Uranus likes to stir things up and keep everyone on their toes. You might think that at least you now know where you stand, but there is an added complication because Aquarius's traditional ruler is Saturn, that most traditional and structured of planets. As a result, the Aquarian man can be caught between the two extremes of Saturnian convention and Uranian innovation. Happily, this gives the Aquarian man tremendous brainpower and intellect.

Some notable Aquarian men, such as Thomas Edison, Francis Galton, and Charles Darwin, have taken things one step further and had insights of pure genius that transformed the world. But even the average Mr. Aquarius, assuming that there is such a creature in this most idiosyncratic of signs, is no slouch when it comes to puzzling out problems and using his intelligence. He isn't always academically minded, because often he considers that to be a waste of time. Instead, he's looking for practical results for everything from changing the wheel on his car to working out the most perplexing mysteries of life.

Mr. Aquarius's emphasis on ideas is accentuated by his air sign, which makes him want to run headlong from the messy business of deep emotions and what he sees as all the fuss that goes with them. He doesn't understand why people can't just deal with the facts of the situation instead of getting heated up about how it affects them emotionally. After all, he's able to be dispassionate, so why can't they? It will be a slightly different story if he has several planets in Pisces, because that means he's much more likely to be swayed by his feelings. Fatherhood doesn't always come easily to Mr. Aquarius, especially if he's governed more by Uranus than by Saturn, but he will do his utmost to give his children a good grounding in common sense and the ability to think for themselves, and will secretly be proud as punch of everything that they achieve even if he can never quite bring himself to say so.

FAMOUS AQUARIUS MEN

Lord Byron • *poet* • *January 22, 1788*
Wolfgang Amadeus Mozart (above right) • *composer* • *January 27, 1756*
Lewis Carroll • *writer* • *January 27, 1832*
Bob Marley • *musician* • *February 6, 1945*
Charles Dickens • *writer* • *February 7, 1812*
Chris Rock • *comedian* • *February 7, 1966*
John Grisham • *writer* • *February 8, 1955*
Abraham Lincoln • *statesman* • *February 12, 1809*
Robbie Williams (above left) • *singer* • *February 13, 1974*
Enzo Ferrari • *car designer* • *February 18, 1898*

THE AQUARIUS WOMAN

Ellen DeGeneres • *broadcaster* • *January 26, 1958*
Oprah Winfrey (above left) • *broadcaster* • *January 29, 1954*
Freya Stark • *explorer* • *January 31, 1893*
Muriel Spark • *writer* • *February 1, 1918*
Charlotte Rampling • *actress* • *February 5, 1946*
Alice Walker • *writer* • *February 9, 1944*
Mia Farrow • *actress* • *February 9, 1945*
Mary Quant • *fashion designer* • *February 11, 1934*
Jennifer Aniston (above right) • *actress* • *February 11, 1969*
Anna Pavlova • *dancer* • *February 12, 1881*

HOW TO SPOT A PISCES

It's easy! All you need to do is to look at their feet, because a Piscean will enjoy emphasizing this part of their body in some way. They might wear beautiful shoes, handmade if they can afford such a luxury, or may go to the opposite extreme and make a point of going barefoot at every opportunity. When standing, their feet may even fall naturally into one of the five ballet positions. There is a dreamy quality to a typical Piscean and often a marked air of glamor, with an emphasis on lovely clothes, floaty scarves, and dangly jewelry. They like to wear perfume or aftershave, too, switching from one fragrance to the next as the fancy takes them. However, some Pisceans take little interest in their appearance, and may even seem to go out of their way to look unkempt and disheveled. Classic Piscean colors are shades of mauve and lilac, aquamarine and sea green.

Pisces
Vital Statistics

ELEMENT: Water
MODALITY: Mutable
PLANETARY RULER: Neptune
COLORS: Sea greens, purples
DAY OF THE WEEK: Thursday
GEMSTONE: Amethyst
TOP TEN TRAITS: Empathetic
• Charitable • Sensitive •
Compassionate • Romantic
• Over-emotional • Vague
• Secretive • Escapist •
Suggestible

THE PISCES MAN

The Pisces glyph shows two fish swimming in opposite directions, and it explains a lot about the Pisces man. He's often slightly confused by life and not quite sure what he's doing, even though he might never dare admit it to anyone. Unfortunately, his astrological inheritance doesn't help in the slightest. He is a water sign, which makes him sensitive to atmospheres and strongly affected by emotion. He's ruled by Neptune, which is the most nebulous and mysterious of all the planets, and which undermines his boundaries. And, just to put the icing on the cake, Pisces is a mutable sign, which makes him changeable and adaptable, but also with strong escapist tendencies. This might sound like a recipe for disaster, yet you only have to scan a list of celebrated Piscean men to see that they can achieve great heights in life in many different fields. Steve Jobs, Rupert Murdoch, Harvey Goldsmith, and Harvey Weinstein were all born under this sign and it isn't only their mothers who admire them for their success.

One characteristic that marks out Mr. Pisces from the other men in the zodiac is his capacity to dream. Some Pisces men make a virtue out of being dreamers and may even manage to change the world in the process. Albert Einstein harnessed the power of his imagination to discover the theory of relativity, with groundbreaking results. Other Pisces men are dreamers who will always have lots of big plans, but somehow never quite manage to turn them into reality. They may give you a string of reasons for their lack of success, often blaming other people or fate rather than themselves. Unfortunately, the slippery nature of the Pisces fish can mean that a few men born under this sign are skilled at double-dealing, playing the victim, or weaving stories about themselves that are completely untrue. It's their way of acting out the Piscean need to escape from reality every now and then. Happily, most Piscean men find more positive ways of doing this.

One of Mr. Pisces's greatest qualities is his sense of compassion. He can be acutely aware of the plight of others, which may prompt him to donate his time or money to a favorite charity or to give someone the emotional or practical support they need. He can also be extremely creative and artistic, and a great many Piscean men enjoy expressing themselves through dance, music, painting, and acting.

FAMOUS PISCES MEN

Sidney Poitier • *actor* • *February 20, 1927*
George Washington • *first US president* • *February 22, 1732*
Samuel Pepys • *diarist* • *February 23, 1633*
Justin Bieber • *singer* • *March 1, 1994*
Daniel Craig • *actor* • *March 2, 1968*
Michelangelo Buonarroti • *painter* • *March 6, 1475*
Jon Hamm • *actor* • *March 10, 1971*
Michael Caine • *actor* • *March 14, 1933*
will. i. am • *musician* • *March 15, 1975*
Rudolf Nureyev (above right) • *dancer* • *March 17, 1938*
Wilfred Owen • *poet* • *March 18, 1893*
Bruce Willis (above left) • *actor* • *March 19, 1955*

FAMOUS PISCES WOMEN

Edna St. Vincent Millay • *poet* • *February 22, 1892*
Emily Blunt • *actress* • *February 23, 1983*
Elizabeth Taylor (above right) • *actress* • *February 27, 1932*
Elizabeth Barrett Browning • *poet* • *March 6, 1806*
Kiri Te Kanawa • *soprano* • *March 6, 1944*
Vita Sackville-West • *writer* • *March 9, 1892*
Juliette Binoche • *actress* • *March 9, 1964*
Liza Minnelli • *singer* • *March 12, 1946*
Isabella Beeton • *writer* • *March 14, 1846*
Glenn Close (above left) • *actress* • *March 19, 1947*

THE PISCES WOMAN

Ms. Pisces has a big heart. Her sensitivity and kindness can be wonderful assets, but they can also act as stumbling blocks when her defenses are down because she's so easily moved by other people's problems. Listening to a friend's tale of woe, reading a newspaper, or even watching a gruelling episode of her favorite soap can be quite an ordeal for her. It's because her powerful imagination makes it only too easy for her to put herself in the shoes of someone who's having a hard time, so she suffers vicariously through them. She can feel equally traumatized by her own problems, which she endlessly replays in her mind until they assume massive proportions that have little bearing on the real situation. This not only gives her sleepless nights, but makes her feel incapable of dealing with whatever is wrong, when in fact she is more than able to cope. It's simply that she believes otherwise. When she does summon up the courage to sort out her difficulties, she feels tremendously proud of herself, and with good reason. However, if she has to stand up to someone and hold her ground, she can castigate herself afterwards about it even if she was perfectly justified in acting as she did.

Dealing with reality in all its light and shade can be a tall order for Ms. Pisces, especially if her chart features several planets in this most sensitive of signs. She has a tendency to push unpleasant facts and thoughts to the back of her mind where, instead of disappearing, they loom at her in a menacing fashion and can scare her considerably. In addition to this, she can be very idealistic, hoping for the best even when it seems most unlikely to happen. It is very common for her to put people on lofty pedestals and then to feel completely let down when she discovers that they aren't the superhuman creatures she imagined. If she has children, Ms. Pisces will think the world of them while doing whatever she can to protect them from disappointments and setbacks, sometimes to the point of being too protective. She will be loving and affectionate toward them, and will use her wonderful imagination to invent exciting games on wet afternoons and restful stories at bedtime. Creativity is very important for Ms. Pisces (the children's illustrator Kate Greenaway, and dancers Marie Rambert, Lynn Seymour, and Cyd Charisse were all born under this sign) so she'll encourage her children to discover their individual talents. She will also teach her children to be kind and considerate to others, and to tune into the more mysterious side of life—something that she herself knows all about.

THE PISCES CHILD

Bringing up a Pisces child can be a delightful experience. They are friendly, helpful, considerate, and affectionate. They do their best to see the good in everyone, and even at a young age have a tendency to tuck waifs and strays under their wing and keep a close eye on them. When passing a charity collecting tin they may donate a few coins from their precious pocket money without being prompted, and they'll gladly let their siblings play with their toys. In many respects, the little Pisces is a model child. However, they do need firm guidance from their parents or other concerned adults, especially when it comes to dealing with facts and honesty. Pisceans sometimes like to manipulate the facts to suit themselves, even to the point of telling half-truths or outright lies, and the young Pisces child must be steered away from this habit. Easily done, you might

think, except that the Pisces child has such a vivid imagination and such a strong attunement to atmospheres that they may be telling the truth as they see it, even if more down-to-earth adults disagree. The world of the Pisces child is often inhabited by fairies, pixies, ghosts, invisible friends,

Star Fact

Pisces's position as the twelfth and last sign of the zodiac has led some people to draw interesting conclusions about reincarnation. They believe that everyone who is born a Pisces is completing their final incarnation on Earth.

and other ethereal creatures. Is the little Piscean telling the truth when they say they've seen such things or are they inventing yet another far-fetched story? The adults concerned must make up their own minds but must also consider the Piscean sensitivity.

The Piscean child is full of emotion that's always waiting to flow out, just like the water sign to which they belong. This means that tears are often never far away, although the child's mutable nature ensures that they are soon followed by smiles and laughter. Creative activities can be very helpful in teaching the Piscean child to examine their emotions instead of being completely ruled by them, and dancing, acting, singing, painting, and writing are all good outlets for children of both sexes.

Procrastination can be an easy trap for adult Pisceans to fall into, partly through fear of facing up to whatever is needed to be done, so the Piscean child should be taught at an early age to reason things out, reach decisions, and act on them. They must be encouraged to do their homework and revise for exams, and also to take responsibility for various small duties at home, such as cleaning out the rabbit's cage, so they begin to discipline their mind and realize that some things simply have to be tackled, no matter how unappealing they might seem.

Star Fact

Pisces has three decanates of 10° each (see p. 21). Pisceans born in the first decanate are idealistic and intuitive. Those born in the second decanate have the tenacity and instincts of their sub-rulers Cancer and the Moon. Those born in the third decanate express the intensity and complexity of their Scorpio and Pluto sub-rulers.

RELATIONSHIPS

HOW THE SIGNS CONNECT WITH OTHER PEOPLE

"'I saw you take his kiss!' ''Tis true.'
'O modesty!' ''Twas strictly kept:
He thought me asleep; at least, I knew
He thought I thought he thought I slept.'"

—"The Kiss," Coventry Patmore

They say that love makes the world go round, but handling relationships is easier for some signs than others. Some revel in being with other people as much as possible while others need a little distance every now and then. For some signs, it is easier to be friends with people than to be lovers, even though they may be in committed relationships.

LIBRA

Partnerships are so important to Librans that they will often prefer to stick with a so-so relationship than to go it alone. Not that they start a relationship expecting it to fizzle out—Librans could teach the rest of the zodiac a thing or two about romance, adoration, and the intoxication of falling in love. It's sustaining that relationship through the humdrum of everyday life that can be difficult for a Libran, because they are so idealist that they are shocked when they discover their beloved is a normal human being after all. Sometimes, they are tempted to stray, simply so they can rekindle the magic of being swept off their feet by a new love, even if they return to their partner when the fling is over. The Libran makes an amusing and entertaining friend, thanks to their innate intelligence, diplomacy and charm.

SCORPIO

Scorpio relationships, both sexual and platonic, are imbued with the intensity that Scorpios direct to every aspect of their lives. This most complex and profound sign is capable of feeling tumultuous love and passion, although their natural caution and secrecy may prevent them ever putting those emotions into words. Every sign needs a partner who understands them but this is especially true of Scorpios, with their tendency to retreat into silence when upset, not to mention the jealousy and suspicion that can taint their relationships whenever they feel vulnerable or uncertain about their partner's loyalty. This sign is often portrayed as being obsessed with sex, and while some Scorpios certainly consider it an integral ingredient of a long-term relationship, others distance themselves from it because it leaves them too exposed emotionally.

Star Fact

The signs that oppose each other in the zodiac wheel (such as Cancer and Capricorn) might seem to be at odds with one another, but in fact they have a tremendous affinity. Each one offers what the other one lacks.

SAGITTARIUS

People are endlessly fascinating to a Sagittarian, and they enjoy collecting interesting friends. The Sagittarian is an amusing, gregarious, and enthusiastic companion, and they always have plenty to talk about because of their vast store of knowledge. They are tolerant and open-minded, so are happy to take people as they find them, but they do struggle with anyone who is dogmatic or who apparently doesn't have two brain cells to rub together. They are a lively and affectionate lover, but their innate need for freedom and independence means they can't bear to feel reined in by a long-term relationship. They need a partner who isn't possessive and who trusts them enough to watch them get swept up in a string of activities without feeling threatened.

CAPRICORN

The emotions that a Capricorn feels and the emotions that they show are often two completely different things. Their natural reserve and shyness, not to mention their fear of emotional rejection, frequently prevents them from telling their loved ones how they really feel about them. Instead, they hope that they'll get the message across in other ways, such as the simple fact of their continued presence in the relationship. This unromantic attitude means they need a partner who can look beneath the surface to what lies underneath, because otherwise the relationship can founder through the Capricorn's apparent indifference. They are supportive friends, although they don't mince their words if they think a little advice is needed, and if they truly love someone they will remain a firm friend for life, even if their work keeps them so busy that their get-togethers are less frequent than they'd like.

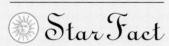

Star Fact

Star signs that have the same cardinal, fixed, or mutable quality can experience tension when they get together, yet they have the same way of dealing with the world so can have very productive relationships.

AQUARIUS

Aquarians excel at friendship. They aren't interested in the color of someone's skin, their sex, or their age. It's their personality that counts, and as a result Aquarians have a fascinating mixture of friends. Although they can be extremely faithful, they will ease friends out of their life with barely a backward glance if they are no longer good company. Long-term relationships can present an Aquarian with more of a problem because they are so easily bored and they hate getting stuck in a rut, even though that's often exactly what happens. Like all the air signs, an Aquarian needs a partner whose intellectual capabilities match their own and who won't try to tie them down. They also require someone who understands the Aquarian need for occasional solitude and the opportunity to discover who they really are with the help of books, philosophy, and kindred spirits.

PISCES

Ah, romance! Pisceans love losing themselves in the excitement of a new relationship, and delight in being swept away on a tidal wave of love, adrenalin, and hope. They need hope because they always believe that their latest relationship will succeed, even if every single encounter in the past has ultimately failed. They revel in the entire experience of falling in love, including being compelled to write poetry and not being able to sleep for weeks, and expect their beloved to feel the same. The doubts will soon start to creep in if their new partner finds it all too easy to keep their feet on the ground. Pisceans are good at friendship, thanks to their sensitivity and empathy, but can sometimes place great demands on their friends when they are going through a crisis. However, as they always reciprocate when the need arises, their friends are happy to step into the breach and lend a helping hand.

No. 14 AT HOME

EACH SIGN'S IDEA OF DOMESTIC BLISS

"O what is more blessed than to throw cares aside, as the mind puts down its burden and, weary with the labor of far journeys, we return home and rest on the couch that we longed for? This alone is worth all that labor."

—Catullus, Latin poet

We all need somewhere that we can call home. Or do we? While some star signs crave the emotional and physical security that comes from having a comfortable home, other signs are less interested in such things and may even relish the knowledge that they are not tied down by too many domestic possessions or commitments.

ARIES

Being at home is great up to a point for an Arian. They enjoy being in familiar surroundings at times, but too much of a good thing will soon start to grate, especially if the Arian thinks their independence is being eroded and they start to feel trapped or taken for granted. When it comes to decorating their home, an Arian likes contemporary furniture that is easy to care for—they have far too many outside interests to spare the time for lots of dusting and polishing. They are drawn to bright, bold colors, and especially shades of red. If they can afford it (and sometimes even if they can't), they love buying the latest technological breakthroughs, such as a state-of-the-art television. Such gadgets may not hang around long, though, because the Arian will want to replace them as soon as there's the slightest hint of them being out of date.

TAURUS

Home offers safety and security to a Taurean. They love the moment when they put their key in the door and know that they are home. It's essential for Taureans to have a roof over their heads, so if money permits they will prefer to buy a property rather than rent one. Their canny financial sense motivates them to look long and hard for a sound investment, even if they have to economize in order to pay the mortgage.

They prefer houses and flats that are traditional, practical, and that, ideally, have a garden because Taurus is a sign that loves being surrounded by nature. Even having a window box and plenty of indoor plants will be better than nothing. They like solid, traditional and comfortable furniture, and have a good eye for relaxing color schemes and tactile fabrics.

GEMINI

When choosing a home, a Gemini needs one that is versatile and adaptable. They want rooms that they can use as the fancy takes them, so they can work in the kitchen one day and the bedroom the next and feel equally comfortable. A Gemini is happiest in rooms that are light, airy, and spacious, with big windows and intriguing views, because anywhere too dark or isolated will gradually make them feel claustrophobic and lackluster. This sign has a magpie instinct and chooses possessions and artifacts that appeal to them, so their homes are often an eclectic mixture of the old, the new, and the weird. You can also expect to find plenty of books and magazines—often gathered hastily into piles that seem in imminent danger of collapse. They are also quite likely to have more than one computer on show.

CANCER

Of all the signs, Cancer has the greatest love of home and family. It is quite common for someone who's strongly Cancerian to stay in the same village or town for most of their life. They may even remain in the same street, either in the house in which they grew up or one just like it. A Cancerian's home is their refuge from the world—a place of familiarity and comfort. When decorating and furnishing their home, they opt for traditional designs that will last, and prefer antiques to furniture that has just emerged from a factory. Cancerians love collecting things, so a typical Cancerian home can be crammed with all sorts of mementoes, ranging from family treasures and photos to holiday souvenirs and all sorts of things that they don't really know what to do with, but simply can't bear to throw away.

LEO

A Leo's home may not exactly be their castle, but it certainly comes close. This is a very dignified sign, so a Leo wants their home to reflect well on them and will spend as much money as they can comfortably afford on making it look good. Regardless of whether the furniture is antique or the latest contemporary designs, it will be comfortable, classy, and may even be the last word in luxury, with deep-pile carpets and sofas that you sink into and can barely struggle out of again. Most Leos are highly creative and enjoy displaying their work, from paintings to needlepoint. They preen like cats when visitors admire their artistic efforts and feel crestfallen and slightly hurt if no one comments on their skills. Leos adore socializing, so it's essential that a Leo's home has enough space for some lavish entertaining.

VIRGO

Virgos are renowned for their neatness and love of tidiness, so it's often imagined that a Virgo home is always the epitome of cleanliness and more hygienic than an operating theater. Although some Virgos can achieve such rigorously high standards with apparent ease, others go to the opposite extreme and are content to live in the sort of mess that would put the average teenager to shame. What is certain is that a Virgo's home is practical and well organized. Being a grounded earth sign means most Virgos are reluctant to spend too much money on unnecessary household items, although they can't resist buying the latest labor-saving gadgets, from bread makers to coffee grinders. Such things often end up gathering dust in the back of a kitchen cupboard once the novelty has worn off.

Ruling the Room

The kitchen is ruled by Cancer and also by the Moon, its ruling planet. Dining rooms and also bathrooms are ruled by two of the water signs—Cancer and Scorpio. Living rooms are ruled by Cancer and Leo. Bedrooms are ruled by Libra and also by Venus, its planetary ruler. Outside, the garden has several rulers—Capricorn and its ruler Saturn, Virgo, Cancer, and Venus. The garage is ruled by Saturn and Uranus.

Venus governs decorating a home to make it look its best. Anyone with a strong Venus in their natal chart will have a flair for interior design.

LIBRA

A Libran's home may be massive or little bigger than a shoebox, but it will be relaxing, attractive, and sophisticated. It is also tastefully decorated in toning colors that are easy on the eye, because most Librans have great taste and shy away from anything too garish or outrageous. They like having interesting ornaments scattered around to act as conversation pieces when they are entertaining, and there are bound to be plenty of books, too. Many Librans are very musical, so they may have an extensive CD collection and might even own a musical instrument such as a piano or guitar. They have a passion for good food and wine, and their love of cooking means the kitchen cupboards are well stocked with all sorts of delicious things to eat, plus some pretty china and beautiful glasses so they can enjoy themselves in style.

ARIES

One of the most endearing Arian traits is enthusiasm, closely followed by energy and optimism, all of which stand an Arian in good stead at work. However, that isn't the whole story by any means. An Arian is filled with excitement when beginning new projects, but they can soon start to flag once the initial buzz has turned into a dull drone and the latest project has lost its sparkle, which means that finishing it can become a real hard slog. It's the day-to-day monotony that gets the Arian down, unless they are fortunate enough to have a job that entrances and motivates them more often than it bores them. An Arian likes to be a leader and initiator, so taking orders from other people isn't always easy for them, especially if they don't agree with what they are being told to do. As a result, they can be happier being self-employed, provided that they are self-disciplined.

TAURUS

When something really matters to them, the Taurean capacity for hard work is almost limitless. They will work round the clock if necessary, although they'll collapse in a heap afterwards and will need plenty of time to recover. Although some signs can't cope with routine, the Taurean finds it comforting because it means they know what they are meant to be doing, so with luck there won't be any nasty surprises. They are happy to work behind the scenes, too, provided that they aren't doing all the spadework ready for someone else to take all the glory—they will feel angry and resentful if that happens. Being an employee is often a better option for a Taurean than being self-employed, partly because they like to have regular money coming in and partly because they love the camaraderie of working with convivial people.

GEMINI

The versatile Gemini can turn their hand to all sorts of jobs and may even switch careers more than once as new enthusiasms take over. Regardless of what they do for a living, it must be something that keeps their brain ticking over like a well-oiled dynamo and gives them a good reason to leap out of bed each day. If it ensures plenty of contact with other people, that's even better because these sociable people really suffer from spending too much time alone. The Gemini is happiest when they are part of a team, so they can bounce their ideas off their colleagues and everyone can reward themselves after a hard day's work with a trip to the pub or favorite restaurant. If they work for a boss, this must be someone whose intellect and talents they respect, otherwise their loyalty will soon flag and they will start looking for another job.

CANCER

Not everyone has the application to work from home, but it's ideal for a Cancerian. These people are often happiest in their own homes anyway, so the thought of working there suits them perfectly, provided that they aren't completely cut off from other people 24 hours a day. Working from home also enables them to switch off with a few domesticated chores every now and then, just so they can keep their home life ticking over. A Cancerian who works away from home with other people needs to feel that these people are part of their extended family, and will soon become the one who provides little treats and who listens to their colleagues' problems. These nurturing and protective qualities make the Cancerian very popular, both as a boss and as a colleague.

STAR SIGN JOBS

Each star sign does particularly well in jobs that make the best of their character and that also suit their ruling planet, element, and modality.

ARIES: construction industry • sports • surgery
TAURUS: beauty industry • gardening • forestry
GEMINI: sales • negotiations • journalism • broadcasting
CANCER: nursing • midwifery • counselling • catering
LEO: entertainment industry • fashion design • interior design
VIRGO: accountancy • banking • insurance • veterinary work
LIBRA: diplomacy • perfume industry • the law • politics
SCORPIO: medicine • psychotherapy • espionage
SAGITTARIUS: publishing • education • travel
CAPRICORN: finance • mathematics • dentistry • osteopathy
AQUARIUS: science • humanitarian work • IT
PISCES: complementary health • dancing • art

LEO

The Leonine capacity for organization really comes into its own at work. A Leo excels at managing other people, thanks to their considerable charm, and enjoys knowing that they are helping to ensure that the office, shop, or factory runs smoothly. However, they must guard against becoming too bossy when people don't do what they are told, and they must also avoid being too grand or egocentric. It's important for a Leo to work with people they like and respect, and it's absolutely essential that they are liked and appreciated in return. Any Leo who thinks they are being taken for granted or exploited will complain vociferously and then look for a better job at the first opportunity. Ideally, their work should offer them plenty of creative and emotional scope.

VIRGO

One of the greatest Virgo motivations is to be of service to others, and this trait is a Virgo's best friend when they are at work. They put every effort into doing their job as best they can, whether it's high-powered or lowly. They will even take this to the point of working overtime for no pay if it's absolutely necessary, although they will eventually complain if the situation goes on for too long. Virgos are particularly good at creating methodical systems, such as organizing the office filing or the computer database, although they get very edgy if they think other people are interfering in what they're doing. Their ruling planet Mercury gives them adaptability, so they can turn their hands to almost anything.

LIBRA

The Libran is such a sociable creature, with a strong drive to create harmonious and comfortable relationships, that they are most content when their working hours are an extension of their social life. Their ruling planet Venus helps them to make friends with their colleagues and they may even have romantic dalliances with some of them, sometimes even leading to marriage. What the Libran needs most of all at work is a pleasant atmosphere and a job that gives their brain some good exercise.

A Libran can't cope for long in a combative or aggressive atmosphere because, even if they stand up for themselves, being perpetually at daggers drawn will eventually affect their physical or mental health. Being self-employed appeals to them but its success depends on the Libran's level of motivation and self-discipline.

SCORPIO

A Scorpio's idea of hell is to be trapped in a job that they don't care about. They need the mental stimulation of working in areas that have meaning for them and the emotional reward of feeling that what they do for a living is somehow making a difference to the world. Their ruling planet, Pluto, draws them to high-powered and intense jobs, although they can enjoy less highly pressured jobs too. They make excellent managers, provided that they can guard against a tendency to be too controlling, domineering, or inflexible because this will soon make them unpopular. Scorpio employees are loyal and hardworking, but they often have one eye on their boss's position because they are convinced that they could make a much better job of it.

SAGITTARIUS

The Sagittarian sense of fun brightens up any workplace. They try to get the best out of every day and encourage all but their most Eeyore-like colleagues to do the same. Their innate optimism also helps things to go smoothly, and if that positive thinking turns out to have been too ambitious, the Sagittarian will laugh it off and immediately turn their mind to what they think is the next big thing coming over the horizon. Despite this bright and breezy attitude, the Sagittarian is quite capable of sinking their teeth into big projects, although they can become a little slapdash once the first enthusiasm wears off. They do well as an employee, a boss, and also when they are self-employed, provided that their social life doesn't interfere too much.

CAPRICORN

Work is an important part of life for most Capricorns. They need a job or an occupation in order to feel they are contributing something to society and also because they yearn for other people's respect. Going to work is rarely a problem for a Capricorn, because they are good at timekeeping and they don't want to incur anyone's anger for not being responsible. It's leaving work each day that can be the difficulty, because the Capricorn tends to be a workaholic who struggles to switch off from their job. Even if they do get home at a decent time they are quite likely to have brought some work with them, either in physical form or as a mental distraction that can come between them and the rest of the family. They always have their cell phone to hand in case of emergencies, too, which makes it hard for them to relax.

Star Fact

A business owner can consult an astrologer for guidance about how their business is faring and what they can expect for it in the future. The astrologer will cast a natal chart for the business, set for the moment the business began. This might be when a shop first opened to customers, when a company was first incorporated, or when one business merged with another. Some of the biggest global businesses consult astrologers, even though they may never advertise that fact.

AQUARIUS

An Aquarian can't help looking at life from a slightly different angle to everyone else, and that goes for their working life, too. They need a job that gives them intellectual stimulation and that suits their erratic nature. It can be conventional or it might be completely off the wall as far as most people are concerned, but their opinions don't matter to the Aquarian. This most friendly of signs will have no difficulties in getting on well with their colleagues and superiors, provided that they have earned the Aquarian's respect. However, if these people fall out of favor or prove that they have feet of clay, the Aquarian may decide that their only recourse is to leave their job and look for more favorable surroundings. Being told what to do can really rub an Aquarian up the wrong way, especially if they think their boss has got it wrong, so they do well being self-employed or running their own business.

Star Fact

Some astrologers work as consultants to businesses, pointing out times of expansion, times when trading is more difficult, and future trends in general. They may also advise on the suitability of prospective members of staff, based on their birth data.

PISCES

Pisceans have a huge capacity for hard work and can really throw themselves into the task at hand, but it often comes at a price. Once the deadline has been met or the job is over, the Piscean will feel emotionally and physically drained and will need time to recuperate. Their innate sensitivity and empathy, courtesy of their ruler Neptune and their water element, makes them very compassionate colleagues, and they like to create an easygoing atmosphere by bringing little treats into work and remembering everyone's birthdays. They can have tremendous intuition and their instincts can guide them in the right direction, but these can never be substitutes for method, order, and organization, all of which the Piscean may have to learn.

No. 16 HEALTH

THE LINKS BETWEEN OUR STAR SIGN AND OUR HEALTH

"Look to your health; and if you have it, praise God, and value it next to a good conscience; for health is the second blessing that we mortals are capable of; a blessing that money cannot buy."

—*The Compleat Angler*, Izaak Walton

Our star sign says a lot about our health and about the areas of our body that need particular attention and extra care. In addition, each star sign has different requirements when it comes to exercise, sleep, and other essentials for a healthy life. Some signs are able to go for long periods without much rest, while others have far less stamina and need plenty of recuperation.

LIBRA

Libra is an air sign, so Librans thrive on mental and intellectual stimulation, feeling sluggish and lethargic without them. However, they are not usually as active as their fellow air sign of Gemini, and with Venus as their ruler Librans do have a strong tendency to take life easy whenever they can. An old astrological epithet is "lazy Libra," which can be rather unfair. Even so, it's a rare Libran who doesn't relish the prospect of a cozy Sunday spent slumped on the sofa. They also enjoy a bang-up meal or a good bottle of wine. Librans can struggle to summon up their willpower and it often vanishes completely when they are confronted by a bar of their favorite chocolate or a slice of cake. They should take care of their kidneys, which is the area of the body ruled by Libra, and may also be susceptible to headaches.

SCORPIO

The typical Scorpio tendency to throw themselves into life with as much passion and intensity as they can muster works perfectly when everything is going well. Their life may be busy, but they thrive on it. However, they can become tense and frustrated if they feel that their efforts are being wasted or they aren't achieving what they set out to do. Another classic Scorpio characteristic is to bottle up their cauldron of emotions. As a result, their thoughts and feelings start going round and round, building up emotional and mental pressure and leading to obsessions and compulsive behavior. They will develop a general sense of dissatisfaction as well as the more specific complaints of insomnia, digestive problems such as irritable bowel syndrome, and possibly even difficulties with the reproductive organs. It will help them tremendously if they can learn to relax, accepting that it is impossible to control everything in their lives.

SAGITTARIUS

People born under this sign are usually very healthy, partly because they love being active. A typical Sagittarian enjoys the great outdoors. Not only do their bodies benefit from the exercise (provided that they don't suffer a sports injury in the process), but being in the fresh air helps to put their problems in perspective. Being very sedentary isn't good for any sign, but a Sagittarian particularly struggles with it and can become stale both mentally and emotionally as a result. Lack of exercise can also lead to weight gain, especially around the hips and thighs, and sciatica. Sagittarians must also guard against eating and drinking too much. It is quite easy for them to overdo it, thanks to their planetary ruler Jupiter, which encourages doing things to excess. However, Jupiter rules the liver, so Sagittarians can become liverish from too much good living and must counteract it with a little moderation every now and then.

The Doctrine of Signatures

Today we have many ways of treating our ailments and illnesses, from conventional medicine to complementary therapies. In the past, medical knowledge was much more basic, and treatment sometimes relied on what was known as the doctrine of signatures. This matched the shape, color, habitat, and growing habits of a plant with the nature of the particular illness that needed to be treated, and was a method of curing like with like. To give one example, walnuts look like brains and were therefore prescribed for ailments affecting the mind and brain.

CAPRICORN

Capricorn is the workhorse of the zodiac, with a strong (or even overdeveloped) sense of responsibility. As a result, it can be very hard for a Capricorn to switch off and relax. If they work for a living, they are quite likely to bring work home with them or to always be on call, so they never have any time off. This can lead to a wide variety of health problems, including difficulties in sleeping and feelings of depression and anxiety. The Capricorn digestion will suffer too, with cramps and abdominal spasms, thanks to their association with Cancer, their opposite sign. Capricorn's planetary ruler is Saturn, which has an affinity for the bones. This means Capricorns must take care of their bones and joints, otherwise they may have problems with arthritis, rheumatism, or osteoporosis, as well as with their posture. Their knees are particularly vulnerable, so need special care. Saturn also rules the teeth, which can be another difficult area for Capricorns.

AQUARIUS

Like their fellow air signs of Gemini and Libra, Aquarians need plenty of mental stimulation for complete health. Being bored or restricted in some way will eventually lead to ailments or even illness. Despite their outwardly relaxed demeanor, the Aquarian is prone to worry, tension, and living on their nerves, so needs plenty of constructive outlets that can help them to unwind. Aquarius rules the shins and ankles, and many Aquarians have weak ankles or find they are easily twisted. Their astrological link with Leo, their opposite sign, can lead to problems with their circulation. Certainly, many Aquarians can easily become chilly, even in the summer, with cold hands and feet. Aquarians are health-conscious, and it is quite common for them to base their diet around moral or humanitarian considerations. For instance, they might refuse to eat meat and fish, or will only choose organic and biodynamic foods.

PISCES

Pisces is such a sensitive sign that very often the Piscean will encounter health problems whenever they are going through an emotionally troublesome phase. For instance, they may come down with a series of colds or they might develop digestive problems, thanks to the link with their opposite sign of Virgo. The sign of Pisces rules the feet, so this is an area of the body that a Piscean should look after carefully. Regular visits to a chiropodist, podiatrist, or even a reflexologist can be very helpful. Facing reality and unpleasant facts can be almost impossible for some Pisceans, who prefer to retreat into escapism. As a result, some Pisceans can struggle with some form of addiction. Pisceans can also suffer from insomnia, because if they are worried about something they will lie awake for hours while fretting about it. Meditation and positive visualization can both be very beneficial.

⊛ Star Fact

Medical astrology states that it is not advisable to have an operation or medical procedure when the Moon occupies the sign that rules the relevant part of the body. For instance, it is not a good idea to have a tooth removed when the Moon is in Capricorn, the sign that governs teeth. Ideally, the tooth should be removed when the Moon is as far away from the sign of Capricorn as possible. It is also considered unwise to undergo surgery when Mars, the planet that rules sharp metal instruments, is retrograde. In practice, of course, this is sometimes unavoidable.

FOOD AND DRINK

ASTROLOGY AND OUR APPETITES

> "Some hae meat, and canna eat,
> And some wad eat that want it,
> But we hae meat and we can eat,
> And sae the Lord be thankit."

— *The Selkirk Grace*, Robert Burns

We depend on food and drink to keep us alive, but they can mean so much more than that. Some signs enjoy eating and drinking so much that these become pleasurable occupations in their own right. Each sign is drawn to specific types of food, which may or may not be good for them.

ARIES

If you want to make an Aries happy, give them something hot and spicy to eat. Being a fire sign, and also being ruled by hot-headed Mars, means that an Aries has a passion for the sort of food that threatens to set fire to their palate.

A typical Arian has a secret addiction to chilies, Indian and Thai curries (usually the hotter the better), and other very spicy foods. Their innate impatience has a lot to do with this, because they need food that gives their taste buds an instant hit, rather than having very subtle flavors. Fast food appeals to them for the same reason, and it also means they don't have to hang around for ages waiting for their food to arrive. Aries is a sign with a lot of energy so Arians like food that will keep their metabolism firing on all cylinders. Although there are vegetarian Arians, most of them enjoy eating carnivorous foods, such as steaks, lamb, and fish. When choosing drinks, they need something with a punchy flavor and a stimulating effect, such as beer, cider, red wine, cherry juice, or orange juice.

TAURUS

It is a rare Taurean who isn't interested in what they eat and drink. Most Taureans absolutely adore their food, often to the point of knowing that they consume too much of it. They particularly enjoy food that is filling, satisfying, and sustaining, such as comforting stews and casseroles, pies, steaks, and roasts. These high amounts of protein usually suit their metabolism, although they must make sure that they have plenty of vegetables and fruit as well in order to get enough roughage in their diet. Sweets, cakes, bread, pastries, and puddings (particularly crumbles and anything chocolatey) are often a Taurean's downfall because they simply can't resist them, regardless of the effect that such treats eventually have on the Taurean's shape. Comfort-eating is a typically Taurean pastime, unless they have very strong willpower. Taureans particularly enjoy drinking full-flavored red wine, and also have a penchant for coffee and hot chocolate.

GEMINI

With their fast metabolism, nervous energy and need to keep on the go, a Gemini is often fortunate enough to be able to get away with eating almost anything while staying relatively slim. They are easily bored, so enjoy food that offers them plenty of variety and is full of interesting flavors, different textures, and a range of colors. Buffets, picnics, and barbecues appeal to them because there is plenty to choose from and they can have a little bit of everything. They also love eating sandwiches, partly because of the variety of fillings to choose from, and partly for speed—a Gemini often has a busy schedule and spends the day rushing from one appointment to the next. Many Geminis benefit from eating a diet that is either completely or mostly vegetarian because they can find it hard to digest dense meat and fish. They enjoy light drinks, such as white wine, fizzy wine, beer, and tea, but can have a tendency to drink too much caffeine.

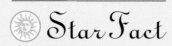 *Star Fact*

Cancer is the sign associated with cooking and kitchens, through its rulership of the stomach.

CANCER

As far as a Cancerian is concerned, nothing can beat a plate of good home cooking. Cancerians have a strong sense of nostalgia and it gives them great pleasure to cook traditional, almost old-fashioned recipes, especially if these have been handed down through the family and remind them of their childhood. For instance, a Cancerian may follow their grandmother's recipe for apple pie or for rice pudding made with the creamiest milk they can find. Love and food go hand in hand for a Cancerian, so providing food for their nearest and dearest is a way of showing their affection. They enjoy eating fish, and shellfish in particular, such as mussels and crab, as well as white meat. Sweet foods also appeal strongly, including gooey treacle tart and cream-filled cakes, especially if they're going through an unhappy phase. Favorite drinks include white wine, milk, tea, fruit squashes, and water.

LEO

The Leo love of luxury is reflected in every aspect of their life, and certainly has a big impact on what they eat and drink. If money permits, they like to consume the best of everything and would rather have a little of something expensive than a lot of something cheap. Although they are happy to eat simple meals, such as beans on toast, a Leo absolutely adores extravagant treats. Smoked salmon, caviar, creamy cheeses, expensive bread, creamy butter, the best cuts of meat, luxury ice cream, and single-estate chocolate will all appear on the Leo menu, and they are so generous that they will gladly invite friends and loved ones round to share the feast. What do Leos like to drink? Champagne, of course! They love fizzy alcoholic drinks because there is something festive about them, so if champagne breaks the bank they will choose prosecco or cava instead. In the summer, they drink Pimm's, cocktails, and good-quality fruit juices, and in the winter they enjoy decent sherry, sloe gin, or gin and tonic.

VIRGO

Ask a Virgo what they eat and they will often explain that they have a limited diet because of their sensitive digestion or their ethical stance on food. However, their innate practicality and caution with money usually prevents them spending over the odds on organic or other special foods. They may like the idea of such things, but they certainly don't like the cost. A Virgo does best on a diet that is high in fruit and vegetables, with plenty of wholefoods such as brown rice and wholemeal bread. They are nervy and often their digestive problems are caused by eating when they feel anxious and tense. It is also important for them to drink plenty of liquids, and especially water. A Virgo is often torn between foods and drinks that they know are healthy and good for them, and those that they know aren't so healthy but that are far more appealing. This can lead to more tension, and also to the typical Virgo tendency of criticizing themselves for what they see as their many faults.

ASTROLOGICAL FLAVORS

Each star sign is associated with particular herbs, spices, and seeds.

ARIES: cayenne pepper • mustard seeds
TAURUS: cloves • sorrel
GEMINI: aniseed • marjoram • caraway seeds
CANCER: verbena • tarragon
LEO: saffron • rosemary
VIRGO: valerian • chicory
LIBRA: cardamom • lemon thyme
SCORPIO: cayenne pepper • paprika
SAGITTARIUS: sage • cinnamon • borage
CAPRICORN: comfrey • flaxseed
AQUARIUS: salt • chilies
PISCES: peppermint • lime flowers

ARIES

An Arian and their money are soon parted, unless they have a strong streak of Taurus running through them. It's all thanks to the Arian's gung-ho attitude and their tendency to rush into schemes and ideas without thinking them through very carefully. If they see something they really want to buy, they will whip out their credit or debit card in a flash. The notion of waiting until they can afford to buy whatever has caught their eye rarely occurs to them, with the result that they often have to steel themselves to open their monthly bank or credit card statements. Despite this, an Arian will become better off as they get older, even if they frequently fail to learn from experience. They are generous with their friends and spend a lot of money socializing. The Arian enjoyment of cars and motorbikes can also work out expensive.

TAURUS

A Taurean really comes into their own when handling their finances. If they are true to their sign they are clever with money, have a great instinct for a bargain, can spot a good investment a mile off and, most of all, have a deep need to know that their money is working hard for them. This is one of the signs that would rather buy their own home than rent someone else's property, and if they are sufficiently flush they will do well investing in property and land. A Taurean likes to squirrel away any spare money they have, putting it into savings accounts that they can dip into if needs be, and this is a habit that can start young. When their finances permit, a Taurean loves indulging themselves with all sorts of treats, but they automatically switch to a more frugal way of life whenever money is tight.

GEMINI

As far as a Gemini is concerned, money is meant to be enjoyed. They have phases of being savvy with their money and making good investments, punctuated by times when the thought of such financial caution bores them rigid and they fall into some bad monetary habits. A Gemini particularly enjoys a lavish spending spree, splashing out on all sorts of things they don't really need but that appeal at the time. Very often, these impulse buys end up being given away to friends or taken to the nearest charity shop, with the Gemini vowing to themselves not to be so impulsive next time. They find it particularly difficult to resist technological gadgets, such as the latest cell phone or an all-singing, all-dancing laptop that they can take with them on their travels.

CANCER

Money represents comfort and security to a Cancerian. This is one of the signs that ties themselves in knots with worry, so it reassures the Cancerian to know that there is some money in the bank, even if they can't help feeling that there is never quite enough of it. When spending money, a Cancerian is always on the hunt for a bargain and they certainly won't pay more than they have to, so may prefer to visit inexpensive shops than temples of luxury. They are thrifty with their own needs and will do without if necessary, especially if they must stretch their finances to pay the household bills or feed and clothe the rest of the family. If the Cancerian has enough money for investments, they like to invest in what they consider to be safe bets that they can also enjoy, such as property, antiques, silver, and furniture.

LEO

It is an unfortunate Leo who has to scrimp and scrape to get by financially because this is a sign that absolutely adores spending money. A Leo revels in treating themselves to all sorts of goodies, whether these are inexpensive or cost a small fortune, but it also gives them tremendous pleasure to buy lavish and generous gifts for their loved ones. They are particularly drawn to upmarket, classy items (or can't-tell-the-difference copies), feeling that anything tacky or cheap is demeaning to them. Leo is a highly organized sign, so they like to keep their finances in apple pie order and pride themselves on never getting into financial hot water, even if they do come perilously close to it at times, thanks to their extravagant habits. Good investments for them include jewelry (especially gold), fine wines, and antiques.

VIRGO

A Virgo definitely knows the value of money and appreciates what it can do. This is a sign that can even choose finance as a career. Regardless of their job, a Virgo likes to make every penny count. They will never pay over the odds for something and will literally go out of their way to secure a bargain. A Virgo has a horror of getting into debt, and may even refuse to have a credit card in order to reduce the chances of overspending. Although they like to look presentable when they are in company, at home they will wear their oldest clothes so they can get the maximum amount of use from them. If they buy something faulty, they have no qualms in demanding their money back, even if they have to be very persistent. When making an investment, a Virgo will go through the facts and figures endlessly until they are finally convinced that they are doing the right thing.

☀ Star Fact

The wallets and purses in which we keep our money are ruled by Venus. However, if we carry our wallet or purse in a bag, that is ruled by the Moon.

LIBRA

Libra loves money. They aren't interested in it for itself, but purely for what it can buy and the enjoyment it can bring. And a Libran certainly knows how to enjoy themselves with the good things in life. They love going out to eat, and will happily visit the most lavish and pricey restaurants they can afford—not so they can brag about them, but simply for what they hope will be a wonderful experience. The difficulty comes in paying for it all, as very often a Libran will blank out any unpleasant information about the state of their finances, preferring to assume that all is well rather than deal with the facts, which may be very different.

When choosing investments, Librans are drawn to paintings, antiques, and other beautiful items. An artifact might be valuable, but if it doesn't look good, the Libran won't want it.

Star Fact

Even some currencies have planetary rulers. The American dollar, for instance, is ruled by the planet Venus.

SCORPIO

Money is power for a Scorpio, not only for what the money can buy, but also for the confidence that having a healthy bank account instills. What is more, a Scorpio will work hard to protect their cash once they have accumulated it by paying some of it into a decent pension, salting it away in other savings, and generally making it work as hard as possible.

They are equally careful when spending their money, not wanting to squander it and always having one eye on a bargain. They like to keep track of the money going in and out of their bank account, to avoid any nasty surprises, and in order to stay in control of their finances. Scorpio is one of the signs that is strongly attracted to status symbols, yet they often begrudge paying a lot of money for them and will scour the Internet for the best possible price. Although they may occasionally make a poor investment, usually they know exactly what they're doing. There are no financial flies on a Scorpio!

SAGITTARIUS

Sagittarians have an easy-come, easy-go attitude to money. They enjoy having some spare cash and spending it on all sorts of enjoyable treats and adventures, and when the money runs out they simply take it on the chin and trust that the financial tables will soon turn again in their favor. Whether things work out like that is another matter, as most Sagittarians have a very extravagant streak, thanks to their planetary ruler Jupiter, and if they aren't careful they can end up with debts that are far bigger than their assets. Even if times are hard, a Sagittarian will do their best to ensure they can still buy what they consider to be life's essentials, which include holidays, books, CDs, DVDs of films, and anything else that caters for their lifelong thirst for knowledge. They like the idea of buying their own home, but are much more relaxed about renting than some signs, as they like the freedom this promises them, even if they never take full advantage of it.

CAPRICORN

Capricorns are renowned as one of the most financially canny and careful signs of the zodiac, and are often caricatured as being surrounded by a cloud of moths whenever they are forced to open their wallets. Even though this is an extreme picture, nevertheless some Capricorns are reluctant to spend their own money unless faced with absolutely no alternative. Others are far more generous, even though they will still draw the line at throwing caution and cash to the winds. They enjoy sniffing out a good bargain, although they are not prepared to compromise on quality so would still rather pay more money for something that will last than opt for what they suspect will be a false economy. This means they can be reluctant to take financial risks and tend to go for established brands rather than anything new and unknown. Food is one area in which they are happy to splurge on some delicious treats, and alcohol is another.

AQUARIUS

The typical Aquarian is slightly revolted by the thought of money. They know that it's an essential aspect of modern life, but financial inequality upsets them and they can become completely incensed when hearing about people who lie and cheat to get what they want. As a result, Aquarians can be wary about making investments and will do their best to check they are putting their money into companies that are ethical and conscientious, and will avoid any that aren't. This is a sign with two planetary rulers, and Aquarians with a strong Saturn influence are highly efficient at managing their own money, priding themselves on keeping track of every penny. Those who are strongly Uranian are more likely to shrug off the fact that they have run up massive debts on a string of credit cards. However, they are very altruistic and humanitarian, and will gladly donate money to their favorite charities, especially if these support animal or human rights.

PISCES

A Piscean knows what they should be doing to consolidate their finances and keep themselves solvent, but all too often the theory isn't borne out in practice. This is especially true when the Piscean is young and without many responsibilities, and therefore feels they have less to lose if they do land in financial hot water. Pisces has two planetary rulers, and those who resonate to their traditional ruler Jupiter will find it much easier to deal with their finances, even if they have to steel themselves to keep a close eye on their bank account and make sensible investments. A Piscean who is more Neptunian will struggle to stay on top of their money, and may even need to be bailed out by others more than once. They will also worry about their money to such an extent that they dare not even think about it because it fills them with dread. When spending their money, a Piscean loves to splurge on fashion, scent, shoes, holidays, and other treats. They will also generously give to others, even when they can't really afford it.

 Star Fact

The financial world is ruled by Capricorn. When Pluto, the planet that governs transformation and the inexorable need for change, first entered Capricorn in January 2008, it coincided with the beginning of the global financial downturn.

№. 19 HOLIDAYS

HOW EACH SIGN LIKES TO GET AWAY
FROM IT ALL

*"For my part, I travel not to go anywhere,
but to go. I travel for travel's sake.
The great affair is to move."*

—*Travels with a Donkey,* Robert Louis Stevenson

When it comes to holidays, some signs are always looking forward to their next far-flung adventure. Yet a few are perfectly content to stay closer to home, and may be so happy with their own four walls that it is a real wrench to leave them. Each star sign has a particular affinity for certain cities and countries, and these can prove to be favorite holiday destinations for them.

trip that is perfectly OK but not great, because that will leave them feeling very disappointed—Scorpios are always looking for intense and significant experiences. This may mean forking out quite a lot of money so they can stay in the best possible surroundings for their budget, although they won't want to waste or squander their money. Some Scorpios will find it hard to resist telling friends about their holiday plans, especially if these might make them turn green with envy. Being a water sign, a Scorpio wilts if it's too hot, but thrives in cooler climates. A lavish skiing holiday, complete with masses of delicious food and drink, is perfect for them.

SAGITTARIUS

Sagittarians are the great travelers of the zodiac so they usually need no urging to take off on a trip. They are happy to venture near or far, provided they will be visiting somewhere that gets them thinking, has a strong cultural or spiritual background, and isn't a run-of-the-mill destination. When they're young, they don't mind putting up with a little discomfort if that's the only way to have an adventure, so they will happily go backpacking or sleep out under the stars if needs be. As they get older and become better off, they like to add a comfortable dash of luxury to their holidays. They do a lot of research before setting off, so they have some background knowledge

of the place when they arrive, and will record their journey with plenty of photos and souvenirs. They may also exaggerate some of their traveler's tales for the benefit of their friends and family.

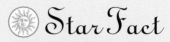

Star Fact

Every country in the world has at least one natal chart, and is therefore ruled by a particular star sign. The charts are set for such events as a country's inception, independence, or an important political act. For instance, most astrologers use July 4, 1776, when the wording of the Declaration of Independence was agreed, as the date for the natal chart of the US. This means the country is ruled by Cancer, the sign of home and family. The UK is ruled by Capricorn (astrologers use the chart for the Union of Great Britain with Ireland, which took place on January 1, 1801), and it is easy to see this sign in the typical British reticence and "stiff upper lip."

CAPRICORN

Holidays and Capricorns don't always go together. Capricorns have such a strong sense of responsibility, often pushing themselves above and beyond the call of duty, that they really need at least one break each year. However, persuading them to take a holiday can be nigh-on impossible. For some of them, going away on holiday is an unnecessary extravagance. Others will find a way of combining business and pleasure, perhaps by taking work with them or visiting places that are associated with their job. If they do go away, they are unlikely to choose a holiday that is extravagant or wildly luxurious, even if they can afford it. They will be much more comfortable with a modest hotel or a self-catering establishment that offers good value for money.

AQUARIUS

An Aquarian's idea of holiday hell is fighting for a tiny patch of sand on a broiling, crowded, and noisy beach. Even if they enjoy people-watching for the first few hours, it won't be long before they crave peace, privacy, and silence. They'll also need some intellectual stimulation, such as visiting a museum or a site of ancient historical interest. Aquarians love to explore the world so will try to visit a different holiday destination each year, especially if it's unusual or off the beaten track, rather than always returning to the same place. They are inquisitive and independent, and don't like being told what to do or when to do it, so dislike having to stick to a rigid holiday itinerary. Aquarians pride themselves on taking as little luggage as possible, but in practice this often means forgetting to pack all sorts of holiday essentials.

PISCES

A typical Piscean lives on their nerves, so a restful holiday is exactly what they need to recharge their batteries. They are instinctively drawn to beautiful surroundings and have a particular affinity for destinations that are near lakes or the sea. However, they need to combine being busy doing nothing with some cultural sightseeing, otherwise they will soon get bored. Pisceans are particularly drawn to places with spiritual, mystical, or magical connections, but can quickly become upset by turbulent or troubled atmospheres. Their delicate digestions mean they should be choosy about what and where they eat, too. Pisceans often enjoy holidaying alone, because then they can please themselves without having to worry about upsetting their travel companions.

HOLIDAY DESTINATIONS

Each star sign has affinities with particular towns and cities, making them good holiday destinations for members of that sign.

ARIES: Kraków, Poland • Naples, Italy • Utrecht, the Netherlands
TAURUS: Dublin, Ireland • Leipzig, Germany • Rhodes, Greece
GEMINI: Bruges, Belgium • London, England • Versailles, France
CANCER: Berne, Switzerland • New York City, US • Venice, Italy
LEO: Mumbai, India • Prague, Czech Republic • San Francisco, US
VIRGO: Crete, Greece • Baghdad, Iraq • Jerusalem, Israel
LIBRA: Johannesburg, South Africa • Miami, Florida • Vienna, Austria
SCORPIO: Fez, Morocco • New Orleans, US • Tokyo, Japan
SAGITTARIUS: Budapest, Hungary • Provence, France • Toronto, Canada
CAPRICORN: Brussels, Belgium • Orkney Islands, Scotland •
Port Said, Egypt
AQUARIUS: Brighton, England • Salzburg, Austria • St Louis, US
PISCES: Chicago, US • Seville, Spain • Valetta, Malta

ASTROLOGICAL LEXICON

Air: One of the four elements. The three air signs are Gemini, Libra, and Aquarius.

Aquarius: The eleventh sign of the zodiac, symbolized by the water carrier. It runs from roughly January 20 to February 18.

Aries: The first sign of the zodiac, symbolized by the ram. It runs from roughly March 21 to April 21.

Cancer: The fourth sign of the zodiac, symbolized by the crab. It runs from roughly June 21 to July 22.

Capricorn: The tenth sign of the zodiac, symbolized by the goat. It runs from roughly December 21 to January 20.

Cardinal: One of the three modalities. The four cardinal signs are Aries, Cancer, Libra, and Capricorn.

Celestial equator: The Earth's equator projected into space.

Decanates: The three sections of 10° each that make up each star sign. The first section is ruled solely by that sign; the second section is ruled by the succeeding sign in the relevant element; and the third section is ruled by the following sign in the relevant element.

Earth: One of the four elements. The three earth signs are Taurus, Virgo, and Capricorn.

Ecliptic: The path that the Sun and all other planets appear to travel around the Earth.

Elements: The four categories of fire, earth, air, and water into which the twelve zodiac signs are divided.

Fire: One of the four elements. The three fire signs are Aries, Leo, and Sagittarius.

Fixed: One of the three modalities. The four fixed signs are Taurus, Leo, Scorpio, and Aquarius.

Gemini: The third sign of the zodiac, symbolized by the twins. It runs from roughly May 21 to June 21.

Geocentric: The astronomical model that places the Earth at the center of the solar system, with the Sun and other planets orbiting around it.

Heliocentric: The astronomical model in which the Sun is at the center and the planets orbit around it.

Jupiter: The planet that lies between Mars and Saturn. The distance between Jupiter and the Sun is approximately 484 million miles (778 million kilometers). Jupiter takes 11.9 years to orbit the Sun. Jupiter rules the sign of Sagittarius and is the traditional ruler of Pisces.

Leo: The fifth sign of the zodiac, symbolized by the lion. It runs from roughly July 22 to August 23.

Libra: The seventh sign of the zodiac, symbolized by the scales. It runs from roughly September 22 to October 23.

Mars: The planet that lies between the Earth and Jupiter. The distance between Mars and the Sun is approximately 142 million miles (228 million kilometers). Mars takes 687 days to orbit the Sun. Mars rules the sign of Aries and is the traditional ruler of Scorpio.

Mercury: The nearest planet to the Sun. The distance between Mercury and the Sun is approximately 36 million miles (58 million kilometers). Mercury takes 88 days to orbit the Sun. Mercury rules the signs of Gemini and Virgo.

Modalities: The three divisions of cardinal, mutable, and fixed into which the zodiac signs are divided.

Moon: The Earth's satellite. The distance between the Moon and the Earth is approximately 239,000 miles (384,000 kilometers). The Moon takes 27.3 days to orbit the Earth. The Moon rules the sign of Cancer.

Mutable: One of the three modalities. The four mutable signs are Gemini, Virgo, Sagittarius, and Pisces.

Neptune: Neptune lies between Uranus and Pluto. The distance between Neptune and the Sun is approximately 2,793 million miles (4,496 million kilometers). Neptune takes 165 years to orbit the Sun. Neptune is the modern ruler of Pisces.

Pisces: The twelfth sign of the zodiac, symbolized by the fish. It runs from roughly February 18 to March 21.

Pluto: Pluto lies past Neptune in the farthest reaches of the solar system. The distance between Pluto and the Sun is an average of 5.9 billion kilometers/3.67 billion miles and varies because of Pluto's markedly elliptical orbit. Pluto takes 249 years to orbit the Sun. Pluto is the modern ruler of Scorpio.

Qualities: Also known as the modalities.

Sagittarius: The ninth sign of the zodiac, symbolized by the archer. It runs from roughly November 22 to December 21.

Saturn: The planet that lies between Jupiter and Uranus. The distance between Saturn and the Sun is approximately 1,427 million kilometers/886 million miles. Saturn takes 29.5 years to orbit the Sun. Saturn rules the sign of Capricorn and is the traditional ruler of Aquarius.

Scorpio: The eighth sign of the zodiac, symbolized by the scorpion. It runs from roughly October 23 to November 22.

Sun: The star at the center of the solar system. The distance between the Sun and the Earth is approximately 150 million kilometers/93 million miles. The Sun rules the sign of Leo.

Sun sign: Another name for a star sign—the zodiac sign that the Sun occupies at the time of birth.

Taurus: The second sign of the zodiac, symbolized by the bull. It runs from roughly April 21 to May 21.

Triplicities: Also called the elements.

Uranus: The planet that lies between Saturn and Neptune. The distance between Uranus and the Sun is approximately 1.78 billion miles (2.87 billion kilometers). Uranus takes 84 years to orbit the Sun. Uranus is the modern ruler of Aquarius.

Venus: Venus lies between Mercury and the Earth. The distance between Venus and the Sun is approximately 67 million miles (108 million kilometers). Venus takes 225 days to orbit the Sun. Venus rules the signs of Taurus and Libra.

Vernal equinox: The moment, on or around March 21, in the northern hemisphere when the Sun reaches 0° Aries along the path of the ecliptic. The Sun is passing from south to north and the hours of day and night are roughly the same.

Virgo: The sixth sign of the zodiac, symbolized by the virgin. It runs from roughly August 23 to September 22.

Water: One of the four elements. The three water signs are Cancer, Scorpio, and Pisces.

Resources and Further Information:

Free charts
www.astro.com/horoscopes

Astrological data
www.astro.com/astro-databank/Main_Page
http://astrodatablog.blogspot.co.uk/

Astrology schools
http://www.astrology.org.uk
http://www.kepler.edu
http://www.londonschoolofastrology.co.uk
http://www.mayoastrology.com

ACKNOWLEDGMENTS

Many thanks to my husband, Bill Martin, for his patience while I wrote this book and to my agent, Chelsey Fox, for her customary invaluable help. Grateful thanks, too, to James, Lucy, and everyone else at Quid who has worked on this book.

PICTURE CREDITS

right	© Getty Images	109	© JaySi	Shutterstock
76	© Elena Stepanova	Shutterstock	110 (and 15)	© Kerstin Schoene	Shutterstock
77	©	Shutterstock	111	© Christine Langer-Pueschel	Shutterstock
78 (and 15)	© Kerstin Schoene	Shutterstock	113 left	© Featureflash	Shutterstock
79	© Konstantin Sutyagin	Shutterstock	right	© Allan Warren	Creative Commons
81 left and right	© s_bukley	Shutterstock	114 left	© DFree	Shutterstock
82 left	© s_bukley	Shutterstock	right	Public domain
right	Public domain	116	© MNStudio	Shutterstock
84	© Serhiy Kobyakov	Shutterstock	117	© Levranii	Shutterstock
85	© Rob Hainer	Shutterstock	118	© Andrey_Popov	Shutterstock
86 (and 15)	© Kerstin Schoene	Shutterstock	120	© Ekaterina Pokrovsky	Shutterstock
87	© vita khorzhevska	Shutterstock	121	© luminaimages	Shutterstock
		123	© Masson	Shutterstock
89 left	© s_bukley	Shutterstock	124	© StockLite	Shutterstock
right	© David Cole	Alamy	125	© altafulla	Shutterstock
90 left	© Featureflash	Shutterstock	126	© iko	Shutterstock
right	©	Shutterstock	127	© Iakov Filimonov	Shutterstock
92	© s_oleg	Shutterstock	128 bottom left	
93	© racorn	Shutterstock	and top right	© bikeriderlondon	Shutterstock
94 (and 15)	© Kerstin Schoene	Shutterstock	129	© Ruslan Kokarev	Shutterstock
95	© Bevan Goldswain	Shutterstock	130	© REDAV	Shutterstock
97 left	© David Fowler	Shutterstock	131	© Creativa	Shutterstock
right	© Helga Esteb	Shutterstock	132	© Alex James Bramwell	Shutterstock
98 left	© Featureflash	Shutterstock	133	© auremar	Shutterstock
right	Public domain	134	© vgstudio	Shutterstock
100	© Monkey Business Images	Shutterstock	135	© Andresr	Shutterstock
101	© Marcel Mooij	Shutterstock	136 bottom left	© Daria Filimonova	Shutterstock
102 (and 15)	© Kerstin Schoene	Shutterstock	top right	© wavebreakmedia	Shutterstock
103	© Mark Winfrey	Shutterstock	137 top left	© Hasloo Group Production Studio	Shutterstock
105 left	© Mr Pics	Shutterstock		
right	Public domain	top right	© Alexander.Yakovlev	Shutterstock
106 left	© Featureflash	Shutterstock		
right	© s_bukley	Shutterstock		
108	© Levranii	Shutterstock		

INDEX